Ivan Moscovich's
MASTERMIND COLLECTION

Sensational Shape Problems
& Other Puzzles

Sterling Publishing Co., Inc.
New York

To Anitta, Hila, and Emilia, with love

Ivan Moscovich Mastermind Collection:
Sensational Shape Problems & Other Puzzles was edited, designed, and typeset by
Imagine Puzzles Ltd., London (info@imaginepuzzles.com)

MANAGING EDITOR
David Popey
ART EDITOR
Keith Miller
CONSULTANT EDITOR
David Bodycombe
EDITORIAL ASSISTANT
Rosemary Browne
PUBLISHING DIRECTOR
Hal Robinson

Clipart: Nova Development Corporation

2 4 6 8 10 9 7 5 3 1

Published by Sterling Publishing Co., Inc.
387 Park Avenue South, New York, NY 10016
© 2005 by Ivan Moscovich
Distributed in Canada by Sterling Publishing
^c/o Canadian Manda Group, 165 Dufferin Street,
Toronto, Ontario, Canada M6K 3H6
Distributed in Great Britain by Chrysalis Books Group PLC
The Chrysalis Building, Bramley Road, London W10 6SP, England
Distributed in Australia by Capricorn Link (Australia) Pty. Ltd.
P.O. Box 704, Windsor, NSW 2756, Australia

Sterling ISBN 1-4027-2347-4

For information about custom editions, special sales, premium and corporate purchases, please
contact Sterling Special Sales Department at 800-805-5489 or specialsales@sterlingpub.com

Contents

Introduction

Ever since my high school days I have loved puzzles and mathematical recreational problems. This love developed into a hobby when, by chance, some time in 1956, I encountered the first issue of *Scientific American* with Martin Gardner's mathematical games column. And for the past 50 years or so I have been designing and inventing teaching aids, puzzles, games, toys, and hands-on science museum exhibits.

Recreational mathematics is mathematics with the emphasis on fun, but, of course, this definition is far too general. The popular fun and pedagogic aspects of recreational mathematics overlap considerably, and there is no clear boundary between recreational and "serious" mathematics. You don't have to be a mathematician to enjoy mathematics. It is just another language, the language of creative thinking and problem-solving, which will enrich your life, like it did and still does mine.

Many people seem convinced that it is possible to get along quite nicely without any mathematical knowledge. This is not so: Mathematics is the basis of all knowledge and the bearer of all high culture. It is never too late to start enjoying and learning the basics of math, which will furnish our all-too sluggish brains with solid mental exercise and provide us with a variety of pleasures to which we may be entirely unaccustomed.

In collecting and creating puzzles, I favor those that are more than just fun, preferring instead puzzles that offer opportunities for intellectual satisfaction and learning experiences, as well as provoking curiosity and creative thinking. To stress these criteria, I call my puzzles Thinkthings.

The *Mastermind Collection* series systematically covers a wide range of mathematical ideas, through a great variety of puzzles, games, problems, and much more, from the best classical puzzles taken from the history of mathematics to many entirely original ideas.

This book includes several geometrical paradoxes inspired by the classic Get Off the Earth puzzle of Sam Loyd. The most famous among these is the Disappearing Pencil puzzle of Mel Stover, which is visualized in a novel design variation. Pythagorean Theorem puzzles, Packing Squares, Fibonacci Spiral, Tangram and other puzzles complete the variety.

A great effort has been made to make all the puzzles understandable to everybody, though some of the solutions may be hard work. For this reason, the ideas are presented in a highly esthetic visual form, making it easier to perceive the underlying mathematics.

More than ever before, I hope that these books will convey my enthusiasm for and fascination with mathematics and share these with the reader. They combine fun and entertainment with intellectual challenges, through which a great number of ideas, basic concepts common to art, science, and everyday life, can be enjoyed and understood.

Some of the games included are designed so that they can easily be made and played. The structure of many is such that they will excite the mind, suggest new ideas and insights, and pave the way for new modes of thought and creative expression.

Despite the diversity of topics, there is an underlying continuity in the topics included. Each individual Thinkthing can stand alone (even if it is, in fact, related to many others), so you can dip in at will without the frustration of cross-referencing.

I hope you will enjoy the *Mastermind Collection* series and Thinkthings as much as I have enjoyed creating them for you.

—Ivan Moscovich

The humble line makes the difference between one type of shape and another. It segments and transforms geometric space and can create surprising patterns.

✳ Dissections and polygon transformations

Problems of dissections must have confronted man thousands of years ago, but the first systematic treatise on the subject seems to be a book by Abul Wefa, a 10th-century Persian astronomer. Only fragments of his book survive, including beautiful dissection problems like:

"Can you dissect three identical squares so that they can be reassembled to make one single big square?"

Wefa's puzzle was the forerunner of one of the most interesting types of geometrical dissections, the problem of dissecting a geometrical figure into another specified figure in the fewest possible number of pieces. Henry Dudeney was the pioneer of this type of puzzle. He solved Wefa's problem using only six pieces. Ever since Dudeney, dissection records have been constantly improving.

There are many ways to divide an area into parts. Some of the ways of making these divisions are particularly interesting.

Putting small shapes together to make larger shapes is also fun—like making a pattern of tiles on a floor.

In mathematics, the combination of small shapes to make larger ones (like a mosaic) is called "tessella-tion," and it has interesting rules of its own, as we shall see later.

The relationships between the sizes of different shapes that fit together also form rules, which are useful for making calculations and predicting other relationships. The Pythagorean theorem is based on an observation of this kind.

If two shapes having straight-line edges (polygons, regular or irregular) can be assembled from the same set of pieces by fitting them together in different ways, then it is clear that the areas of the two figures are the same.

Conversely, it can also be shown that any two polygons of equal area may be dissected into a finite number of pieces that may be assembled to form either of the two original polygons.

The main interest of dissections as recreational math problems is to find how to dissect one figure into another using the *minimal* number of pieces. The branch of mathematics called *dissection theory* provides valuable insights into the solutions of many practical problems in plane and solid geometry.

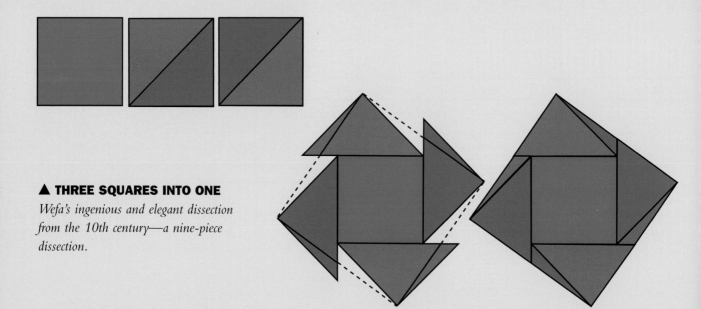

▲ THREE SQUARES INTO ONE
Wefa's ingenious and elegant dissection from the 10th century—a nine-piece dissection.

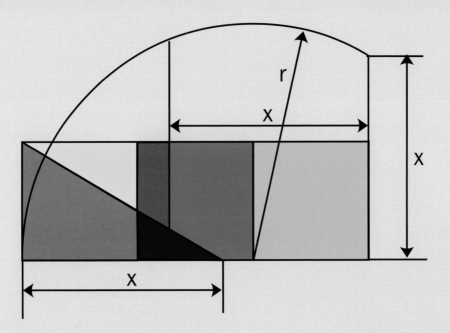

▲ **THREE SQUARES INTO ONE**
Dudeney's dissection, improving Wefa's dissection, using only six pieces to achieve the solution.

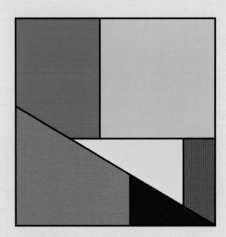

❋ More dissections and polygon transformations

In dissection problems, the pieces may already be given; the object then is to create as many interesting patterns as possible with them. The ancient recreation of tangrams is a good example.

On the other hand, two undissected polygons may be given; then the problem is to find ways to dissect them to transform one into the other. Usually the object is to use as few pieces as possible.

A third, apparently paradoxical, variant is to dissect a shape into pieces, remove one piece, and reassemble the remainder to form the original shape. Although this is impossible, many puzzles appear to achieve it.

It's one thing to cut up a shape or pattern but quite another to coordinate the result. Sometimes it only requires common sense but often it involves careful planning and skill.

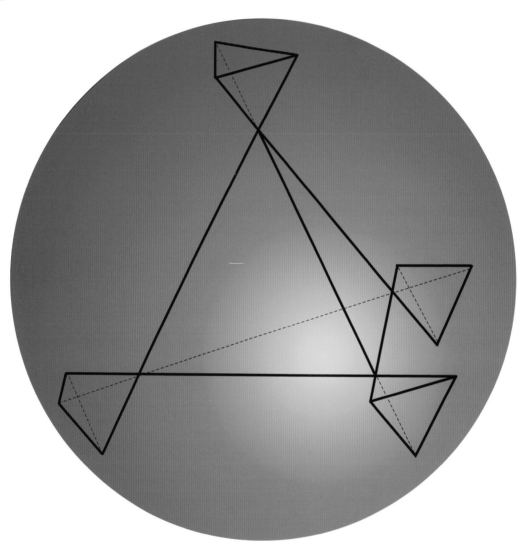

▲ DISSECTING SPACE

Imagine a tetrahedron with its four vertices placed inside a sphere. (The vertices do not touch the edge of the sphere.)

The sphere is cut with four plane cuts exactly along the four sides of the tetrahedron, dividing the sphere into a number of separate parts.

How many?

ANSWER: PAGE 98

▲ SQUARE CAKE

The object is to cut the square cake, frosted and decorated on top and around the four sides, into five pieces of equal volume and with equal amounts of frosting.

If there were no frosting or decorations, it would be simple to cut the cake with four straight parallel cuts, but here the problem is a bit more difficult, since that would give two of the pieces much more of the red frosting.

ANSWER: PAGE 98

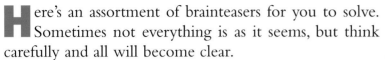

Here's an assortment of brainteasers for you to solve. Sometimes not everything is as it seems, but think carefully and all will become clear.

▲ CONSECUTIVE WATERMELONS

Seven large watermelons have weights (in kilograms) of consecutive odd numbers, with their weights averaging seven kilograms.

What is the weight of the heaviest watermelon?

ANSWER: PAGE 98

▲ FALLING BRICK

How much does the brick falling on the bricklayer's head weigh, if it weighs 1 kilogram plus the weight of half the brick?

ANSWER: PAGE 98

▼ T-TIME

Can you put the four pieces together to create a perfect capital letter "T" and all the other figures below?

ANSWER: PAGE 99

Tangrams originally caused great consternation in some countries. The French called them "Chinese headbreakers" while English newspapers wondered why children puzzled over such shapes for hours at a time.

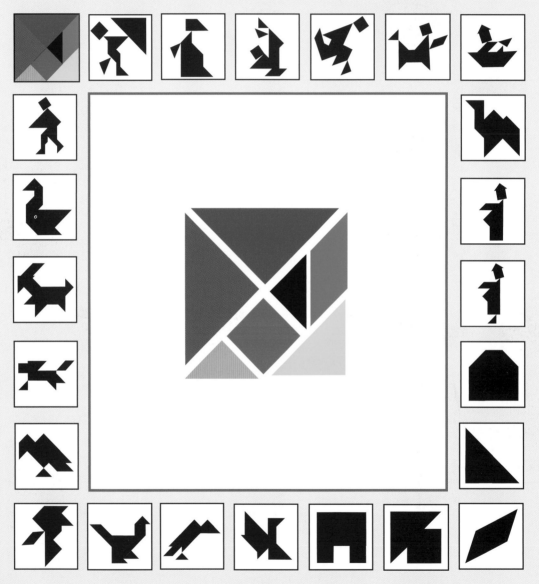

▲ TANGRAM

The oldest known mathematical dissection puzzle is the Chinese tangram. The tangram in its classical form is one of the world's most beautiful puzzles. Its earliest known reference is in a Chinese book published in 1826, but it may have originated much earlier.

Copy and cut out the seven colored tangram pieces.
After you have solved all the puzzles shown here, try to create your own designs and figures.
ANSWER: PAGE 99

▲ TANGRAM NUMBERS

Numbers 8 and 0 are missing. After reconstructing the above numbers, try experimenting to create the best 8 and 0 you can make from the seven tangram pieces.

ANSWER: PAGE *100*

Perhaps the puzzles on these pages will help you to realize the remarkable flexibility of the pieces that make up the tangram square. And they're portable too!

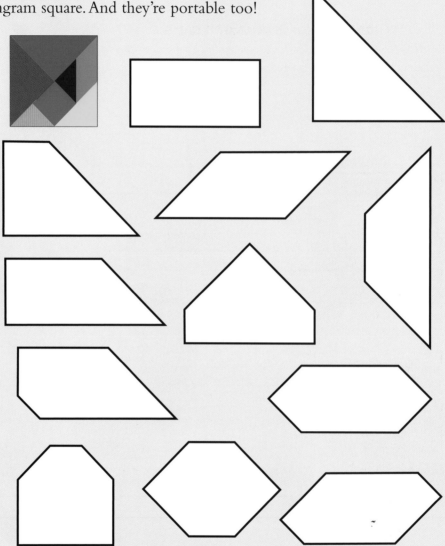

▲ TANGRAM POLYGONS

Two Chinese mathematicians, Fu Wang and Chuan-Hsiung, proved that using the seven tangram pieces only 13 different convex polygons can be formed: one triangle, six quadrilaterals, two pentagons, and four hexagons.

The outlines of the 13 convex polygons are shown above.

You've already seen the square. Can you make the other twelve shapes out of the set of seven tangram pieces?

ANSWER: PAGE 100

TANGRAM POLYGONS PACKING GAME 1

The area of the 11-by-11 square is just a bit more than that of the 13 polygons on the opposite page. How many of the polygons can you pack in this square?

ANSWER: PAGE 101

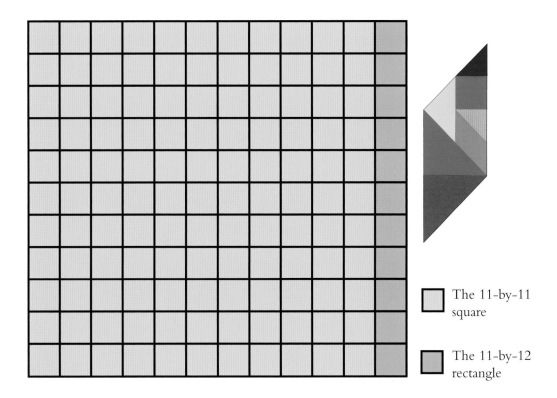

☐ The 11-by-11 square

☐ The 11-by-12 rectangle

TANGRAM POLYGONS PACKING GAME 2

How many can you pack in the 11-by-12 rectangle?

ANSWER: PAGE 101

▲ TANGRAM PARADOXES

All the figures on this page were created using the seven tangram pieces.
  Can you solve the puzzles to explain the small differences between them?
  (The paradoxical tangram problems are included in The Tangram Book, *by Jerry Slocum, collected from China, France, and Sam Loyd's, Henry Dudeney's, and Gianni Sarcone's books.)*

ANSWER: PAGE 101

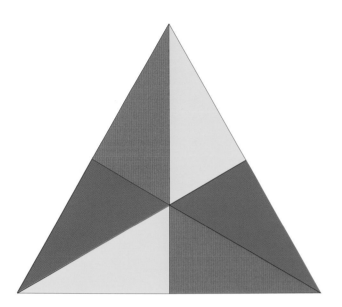

◀ TRIANGLE TANGRAM

Dividing an equilateral triangle into six identical triangles having angles of 30, 60, and 90 degrees, we get a set of pieces that can be joined into a surprising number of shapes.

Can you solve the three outline puzzles below and create similar puzzles of your own design?

ANSWER: PAGE 102

There are many shapes and objects that can make interesting tangram-style puzzles—chessboards or the tiles on your kitchen floor, for instance. However, please remember to ask permission before cutting up, say, the family's morning newspaper!

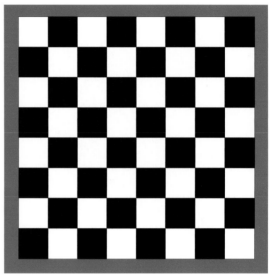

▶ CHESSBOARD DISSECTION
This is a classic by Henry Dudeney (see page 39). He dissected a chessboard, forming a sentence as shown below, with a dot after each word.

Can you recreate Dudeney's chessboard?

ANSWER: PAGE 102

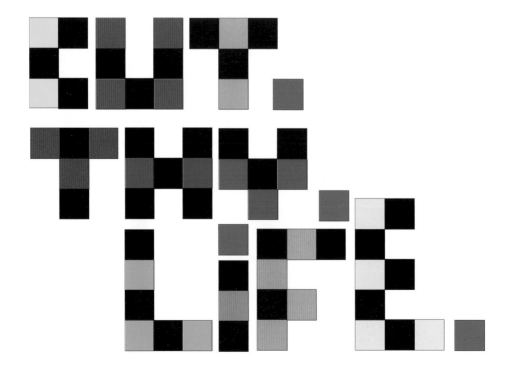

▲ PENTAGONAL STAR

Using the six right-angled triangles above, can you make the five-pointed star shown at the top of the page?

Then, using the same pieces, can you form a six-pointed star (resembling a cowboy's spur)?

ANSWER: PAGE 102

Why not have a tangram with curves—it makes for more shapely drawings and provides an array of new constructions at the same time. Go on, put your heart into it!

▲ HEART TANGRAM

Use the nine pieces of the heart tangram to form each of the two silhouettes.

Try creating your own designs and puzzles.

ANSWER: PAGE *103*

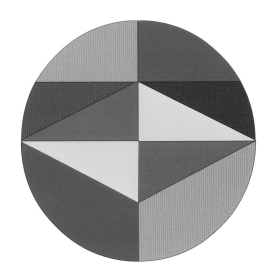

◄ CIRCLE TANGRAM

Use the 10 pieces of the circle tangram to form each of the two silhouettes. Pieces may be flipped.

What other designs can you come up with?

ANSWER: PAGE *103*

Whether dividing a quadrilateral into two triangles or six triangles, there's always a way to get a puzzle out of it.

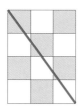

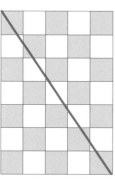

3-by-4 rectangle:
6 squares crossed

5-by-7 rectangle:
11 squares crossed

10-by-14 rectangle: ?

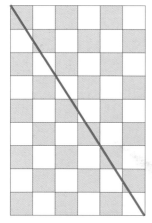

6-by-9 rectangle:
12 squares crossed

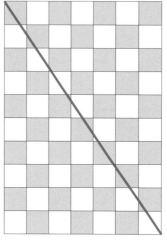

7-by-10 rectangle:
16 squares crossed

▲ DIAGONAL CROSSING

Diagonals have been drawn in rectangular grids. How many squares in each grid are crossed by the diagonals?

How many squares in the 10-by-14 rectangle will be crossed by the diagonal?

Can you generalize the problem and work out the general rule for any rectangle?

ANSWER: PAGE **104**

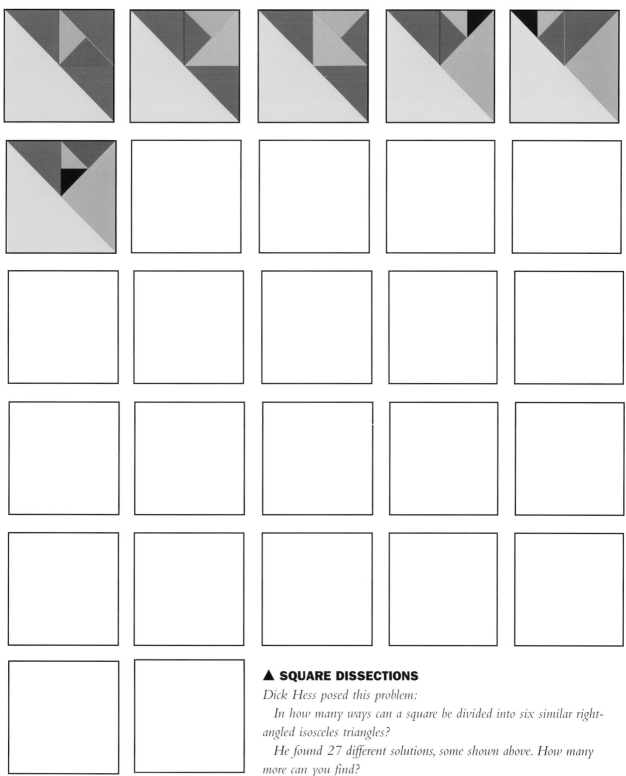

▲ SQUARE DISSECTIONS

Dick Hess posed this problem:

In how many ways can a square be divided into six similar right-angled isosceles triangles?

He found 27 different solutions, some shown above. How many more can you find?

ANSWER: PAGE 105

Forces act on us every day. For example, gravity keeps our feet firmly on the ground, and scales represent this force as weight in pounds. The willpower not to eat too many cupcakes is another type of force and the two forces are often linked!

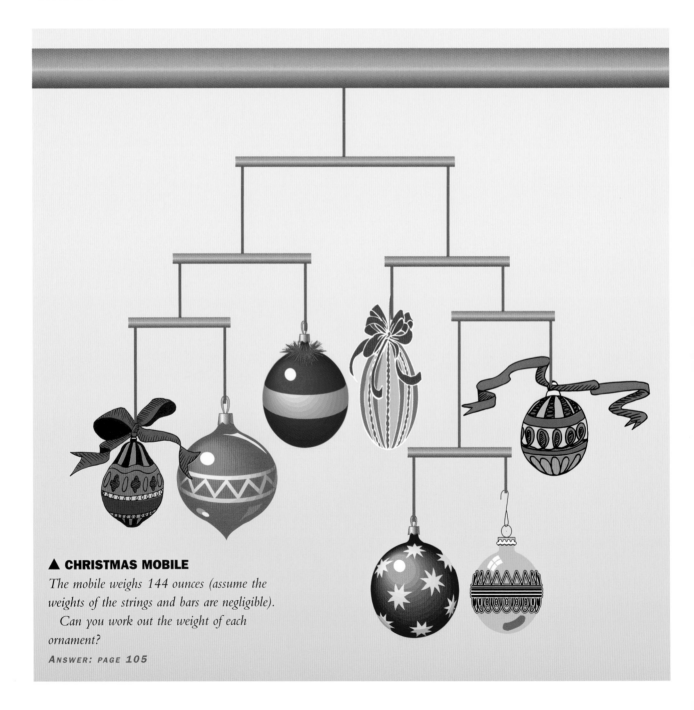

▲ CHRISTMAS MOBILE

The mobile weighs 144 ounces (assume the weights of the strings and bars are negligible).

Can you work out the weight of each ornament?

ANSWER: PAGE *105*

✳ Parallelogram of forces

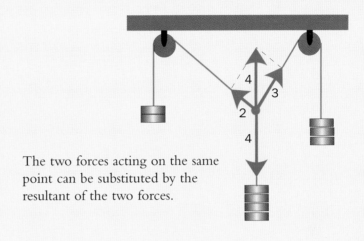

The two forces acting on the same point can be substituted by the resultant of the two forces.

The illustration, above left, is from the title page of *The Elements of the Art of Weighing* by Simon Stevin (1548–1620), which features the famous "wreath of spheres."

One of Stevin's most famous discoveries, of which he was quite proud, was the proof that when weights are in equilibrium on an inclined plane, the weights of the bodies involved are proportional to the lengths of the planes. Stevin proved this by using an ingenious geometrical argument. He considered the picture on his title page with the "wreath of spheres," a necklace of metal spheres.

His argument was that everything should be in equilibrium, for otherwise one would have "something that moves," i.e., a perpetual motion machine. Now leave out the "free" balls hanging in the air; the system that remains is in equilibrium. Count the balls on the inclining plane, and you have the above law!

This was due to the relationship between the downward forces on either side being in equilibrium, due to the differing angle of their support. Such a resolution of forces is known today as the *parallelogram of forces*.

The parallelogram of forces can be used to calculate the resultant (combined effect) of two different forces acting together on an object. The two forces are represented by two lines drawn at an angle to each other. By completing the parallelogram of which the two lines are sides, a diagonal may be drawn from the original angle to the opposite corner to represent the resultant force vector.

Above the illustration of this experiment Stevin placed his scientific motto:
"*Nothing is the miracle it appears to be.*"

▶ **FORCE FOUR**

Four forces are acting on a point (blue). The sizes of the forces are denoted in kilograms.

Can you work out the size of the resultant force?

ANSWER: PAGE *106*

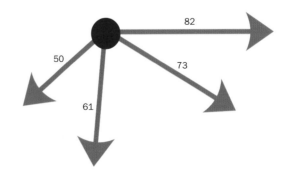

Weighty problems are usually the domain of world leaders and Olympic weight lifters. However, now it's time to take some of the strain onto your own shoulders—so get solving!

▶ THREE WEIGHTS

You have three identically shaped boxes of different weights.

With one set of scales, how many weighings will you need to arrange the three boxes from the lightest to the heaviest?

ANSWER: PAGE 106

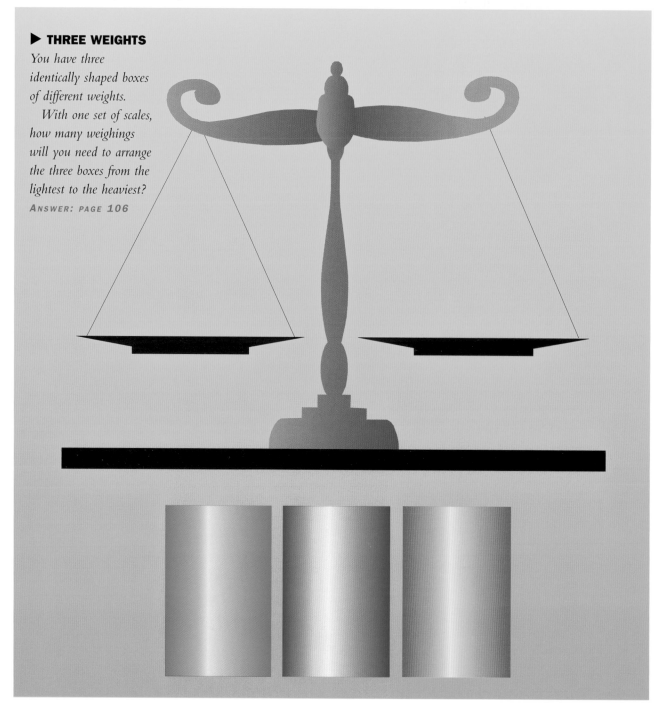

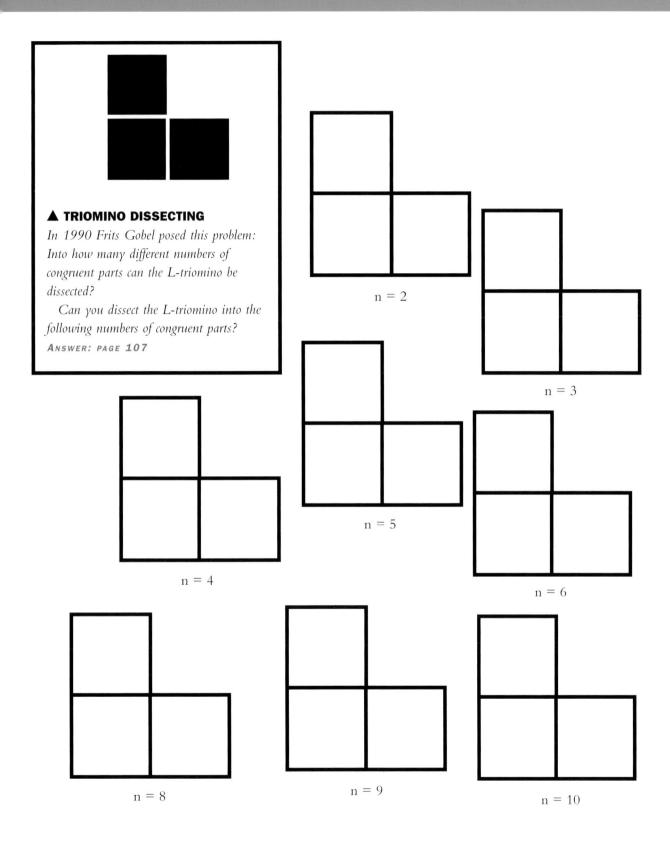

▲ TRIOMINO DISSECTING

In 1990 Frits Gobel posed this problem: Into how many different numbers of congruent parts can the L-triomino be dissected?

Can you dissect the L-triomino into the following numbers of congruent parts?

ANSWER: PAGE 107

n = 2

n = 3

n = 5

n = 4

n = 6

n = 8

n = 9

n = 10

Did you know that there's more than one way to quarter a square? Maybe you could try one of these patterns the next time a birthday party gets a little boring. Oddly shaped cake slices should liven things up.

❋ Dissection into equal parts

When we are dealing with problems of dissecting shapes to produce pieces of equal size, we are dealing with fractions and with the idea of congruency—shapes that are of the same shape. Of course, shapes of the same size (area) do not have to be the same shape!

Some of these problems may be very tricky, because congruent shapes can appear in different orientations, and in trying to solve dissection puzzles, ideas of both reflective and rotational symmetry have to be used.

▼ QUARTERING SQUARES

There are 37 different ways to dissect a 6-by-6 square grid into four identical congruent parts (quarters) along the grid lines. (Rotations and reflections are not considered different.) Can you find them all?

ANSWER: PAGE 108

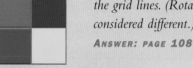

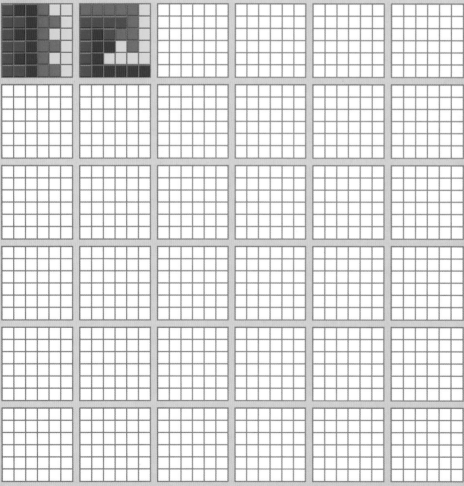

▼ BOMB DEMOLITION EXPERT

The clock is ticking and you have to defuse the bomb before it explodes by cutting its wiring into two parts, from the bottom blue wires to the top green wires, through the interconnecting mesh of red wires, and with as few cuts as possible. You may only cut through the wires, and not at the connection points. Quick! Before the bomb explodes!

ANSWER: PAGE 108

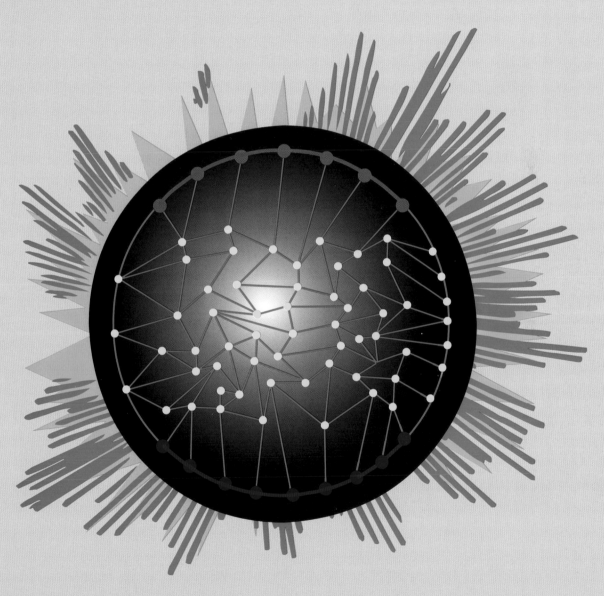

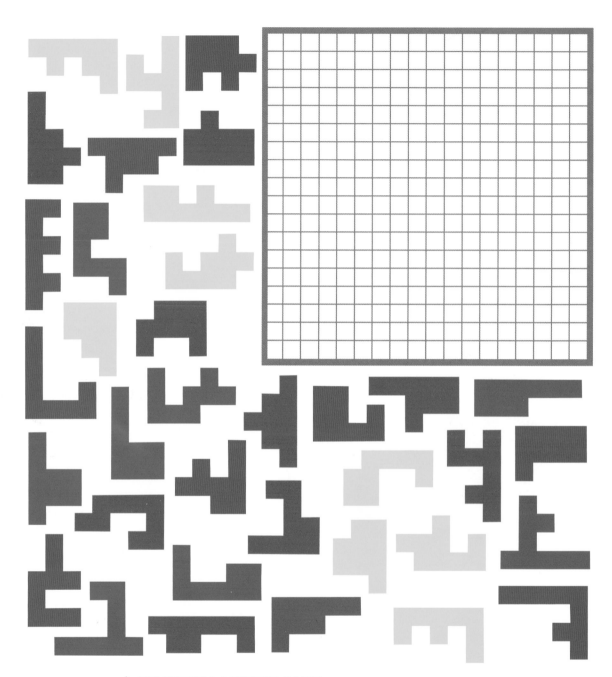

▲ QUARTERING SQUARES GAME

The set of 36 non-congruent quarters that results from quartering a 6-by-6 square (excluding the square 3-by-3 quarter) occupies an area of 324 unit squares, which is the area of an 18-by-18 square, our gameboard.

Can you cover this square using the 36 shapes?

ANSWER: PAGE *109*

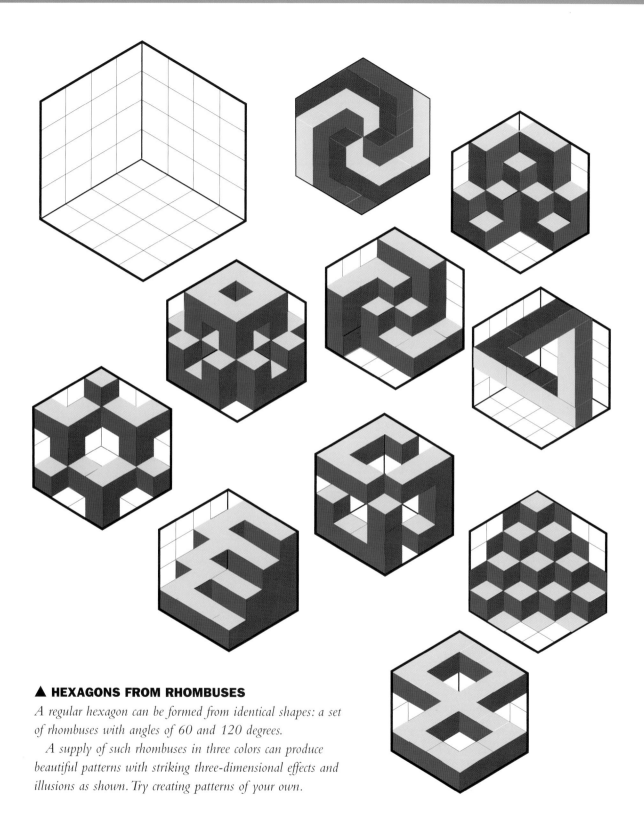

▲ HEXAGONS FROM RHOMBUSES

A regular hexagon can be formed from identical shapes: a set of rhombuses with angles of 60 and 120 degrees.

A supply of such rhombuses in three colors can produce beautiful patterns with striking three-dimensional effects and illusions as shown. Try creating patterns of your own.

Here's a good way to think about a rhombus: remember that a rhombus is to a parallelogram as the square is to the rectangle. The diagonals are perpendicular to one another and all four sides are equal lengths.

▶ DODECAGONS FROM RHOMBUSES

A regular dodecagon can be dissected into rhombuses, all of them having sides of the same length. Any such dissection will always include three types of rhombuses: 6 wide ones, 6 narrow ones, and 3 squares, for a total of 15 pieces. Four such dissections are shown, but there are many more.

The three rhombuses have a simple relationship—increasing one set of angles and reducing the other by 30 degrees gives you the next rhombus:

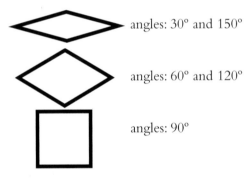

angles: 30° and 150°

angles: 60° and 120°

angles: 90°

The parts of four dodecagons can be fitted together in many different ways to make one large dodecagon consisting of 60 rhombuses, as shown at the top of the opposite page.

Can you find more?

ANSWER: PAGE 109

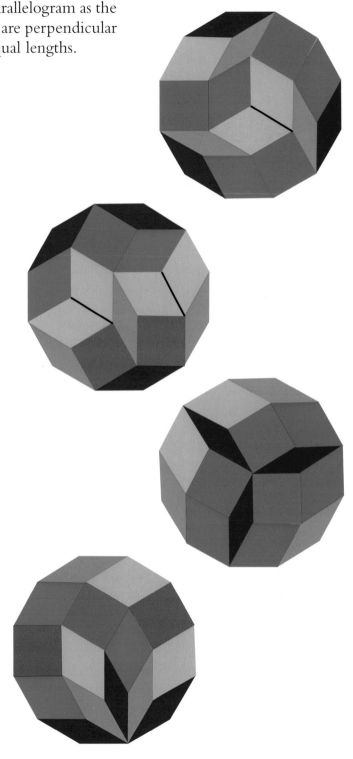

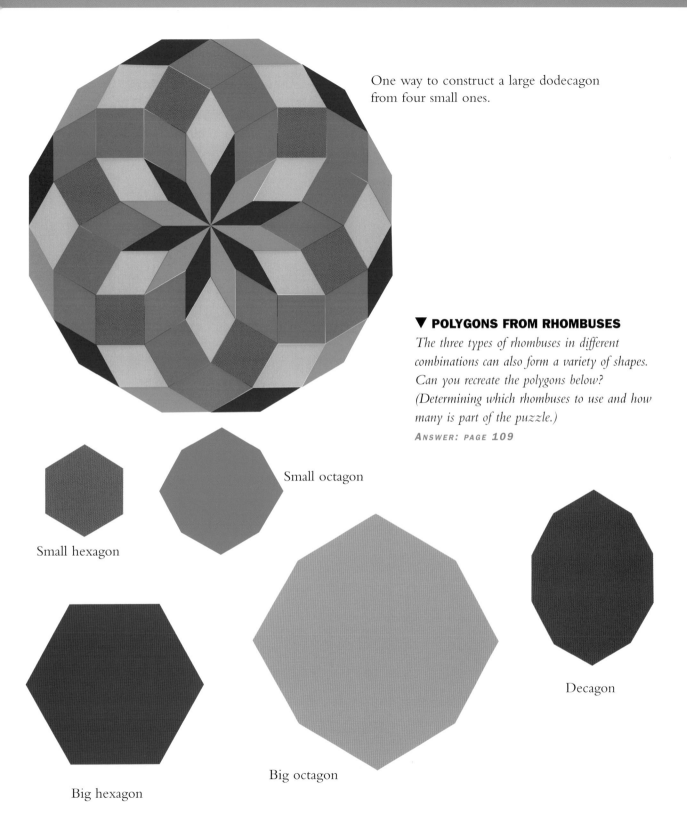

One way to construct a large dodecagon from four small ones.

▼ POLYGONS FROM RHOMBUSES

The three types of rhombuses in different combinations can also form a variety of shapes. Can you recreate the polygons below? (Determining which rhombuses to use and how many is part of the puzzle.)

ANSWER: PAGE *109*

Small hexagon

Small octagon

Big hexagon

Big octagon

Decagon

Each regular polygon has a different number of ways in which it can be dissected into equal parts. See how you fare with the hexagon below.

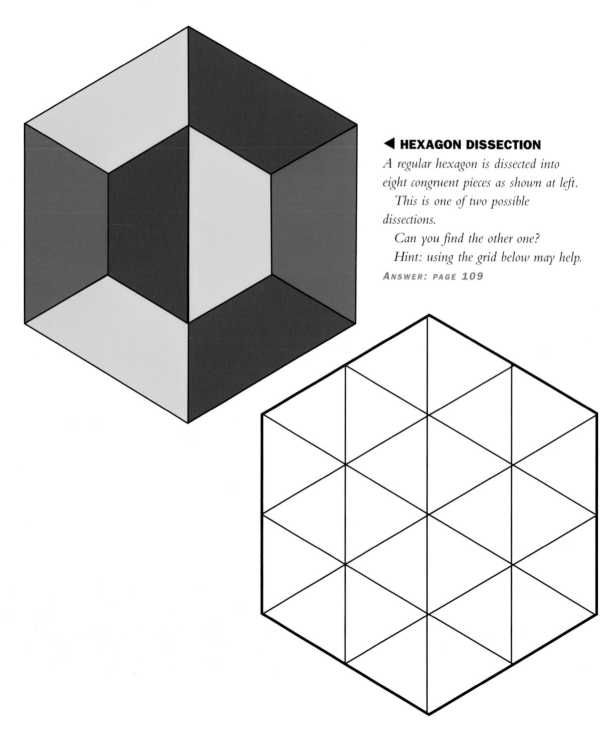

◄ HEXAGON DISSECTION

A regular hexagon is dissected into eight congruent pieces as shown at left.

This is one of two possible dissections.

Can you find the other one?

Hint: using the grid below may help.

ANSWER: PAGE 109

▼ TWENTY-ONE WEIGHTS

You have 21 identical boxes, one of which is slightly heavier than the rest.
  With one balance scale, how many weighings will you need to identify
the heavier box?

ANSWER: PAGE 109

Gravity can be summed up according to the well-worn phrase "what goes up must come down." If it hadn't been an apple that Newton observed it could well have been a cannonball.

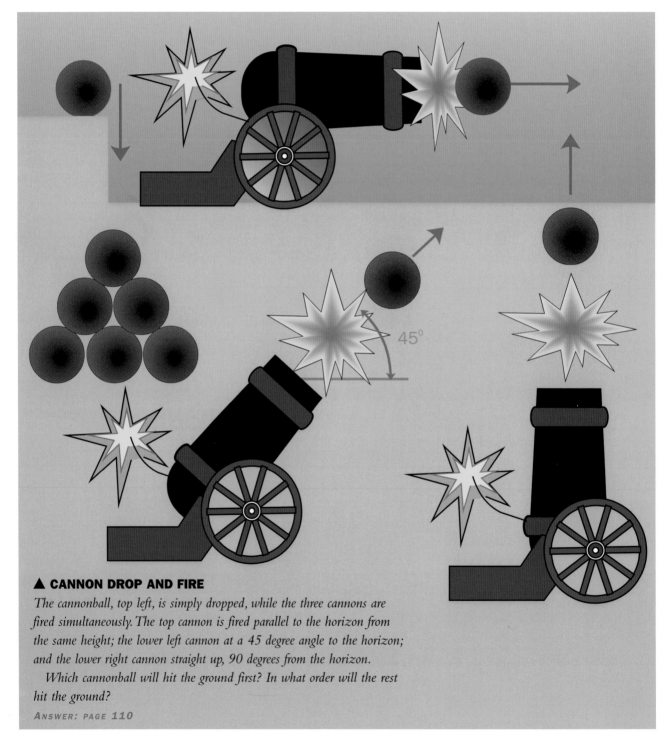

▲ CANNON DROP AND FIRE

The cannonball, top left, is simply dropped, while the three cannons are fired simultaneously. The top cannon is fired parallel to the horizon from the same height; the lower left cannon at a 45 degree angle to the horizon; and the lower right cannon straight up, 90 degrees from the horizon.

Which cannonball will hit the ground first? In what order will the rest hit the ground?

ANSWER: PAGE 110

We don't know anything. Everything about gravity is mysterious.
Michael Nieto, theoretical physicist at Los Alamos National Lab, New Mexico

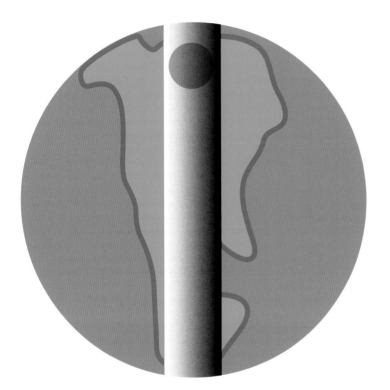

◄ **GRAVITY FALL**

What would happen if you drilled a hole from the North Pole to the South Pole and then dropped a heavy ball into the hole? (Ignore friction and air resistance.)

ANSWER: PAGE **110**

✳ Gravity and the famous apple

Gravity was discovered by the British scientist Isaac Newton (1643–1727) after he saw an apple fall off a tree, or so the story goes.

What Newton concluded from the incident was that the force that makes the Moon orbit the Earth, and the planets orbit the Sun, is actually the same as the force that made the apple fall to the Earth. How?

Objects attract each other. Usually the attraction is so small that it can't be noticed.

However, when the object is as big as the Earth, it is capable of attracting other objects, even as big as the Moon. The Earth is much larger and heavier than the Moon, so the Moon is kept in the Earth's orbit due to gravity. If gravity is capable of keeping the Moon within its orbit, what effect do you think it would have on an itsy-bitsy little apple? It certainly would attract it like a magnet attracts a pin—powerfully!

Think of the puzzles on these pages as complicated tangram variations where the pieces can be reassembled from one shape into another. See how long it takes you to become the star of the show.

▲ SQUARE TO STAR

A square has been dissected into six pieces as shown.

Copy and cut out the six pieces to form a regular six-pointed star.

ANSWER: PAGE 110

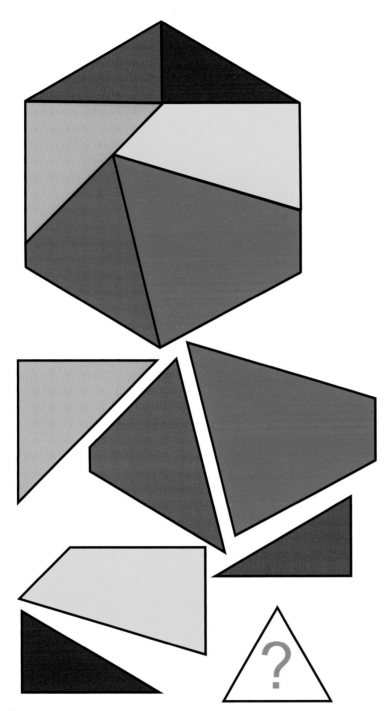

▲ HEXAGON TO TRIANGLE

Copy and cut out the pieces of the dissected hexagon.

Can you find a way to arrange the six pieces of the dissected hexagon to form an equilateral triangle?

ANSWER: PAGE 110

Henry Dudeney (1857–1930)

Henry Dudeney was England's greatest inventor of puzzles; indeed, he may well have been the greatest puzzlemaker who ever lived.

Today there is scarcely a single puzzle book that does not contain (often without credit) dozens of brilliant mathematical problems that had their origin in Dudeney's fertile imagination.

He was born in the village of Mayfield in 1857. Thus he was 16 years younger than Sam Loyd (1841–1911), the American puzzle genius. In the 1890s they collaborated on a series of puzzle articles for the magazine Tit-Bits, *and later they arranged to exchange puzzles for their magazine and newspaper columns. This may explain the large amount of duplication in the published writings of Loyd and Dudeney. Of the two, Dudeney was probably the better mathematician. Loyd excelled in catching the public fancy with manufactured toys and advertising novelties. Dudeney's work was more mathematically sophisticated. Like Loyd he enjoyed clothing his problems with amusing anecdotes.*

Dudeney's first book, The Canterbury Puzzles, *was published in 1907.*

Although he only had a basic education, he had a particular interest in mathematics. Dudeney worked as a clerk in the Civil Service from the age of 13, but continued to study mathematics and its history in his spare time.

His very popular collection of mathematical puzzles, Modern Puzzles, *was published in 1926.*

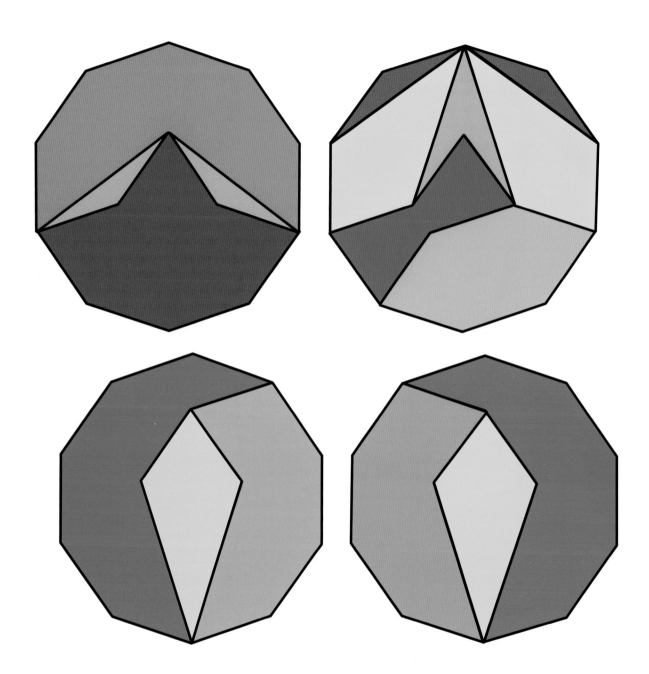

▲ PENTAGONAL STAR

Copy the four decagons and cut them into the 17 parts shown. Can you then rearrange the parts to make a regular five-pointed star?

  (courtesy of Greg N. Frederickson)

ANSWER: PAGE 110

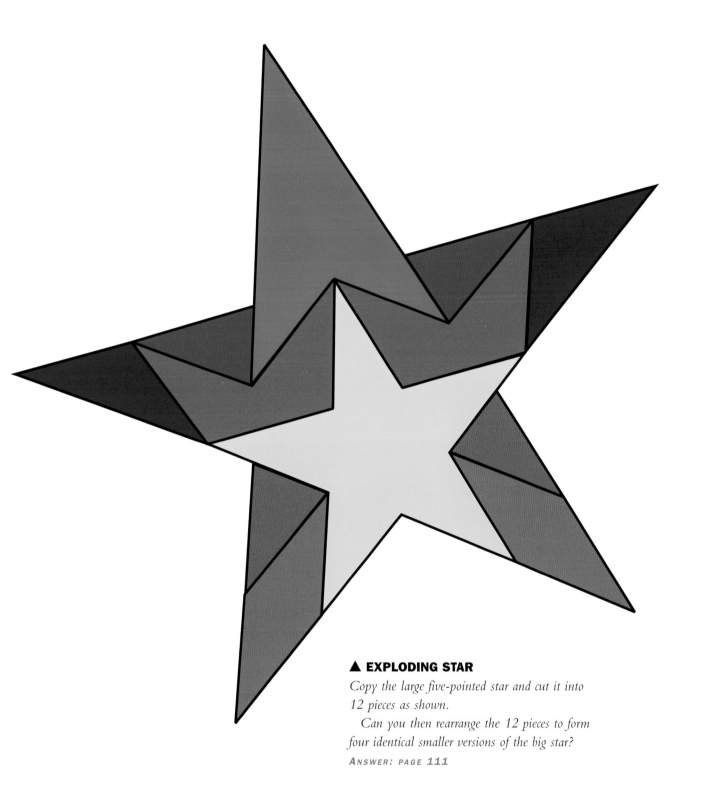

▲ EXPLODING STAR

Copy the large five-pointed star and cut it into 12 pieces as shown.

Can you then rearrange the 12 pieces to form four identical smaller versions of the big star?

ANSWER: PAGE 111

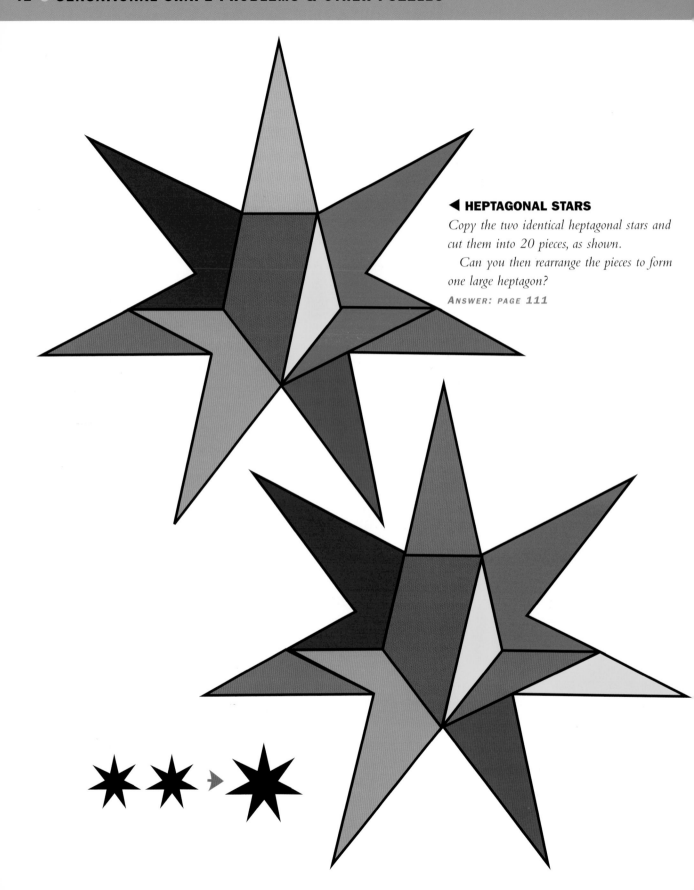

◄ HEPTAGONAL STARS

Copy the two identical heptagonal stars and cut them into 20 pieces, as shown.

Can you then rearrange the pieces to form one large heptagon?

ANSWER: PAGE **111**

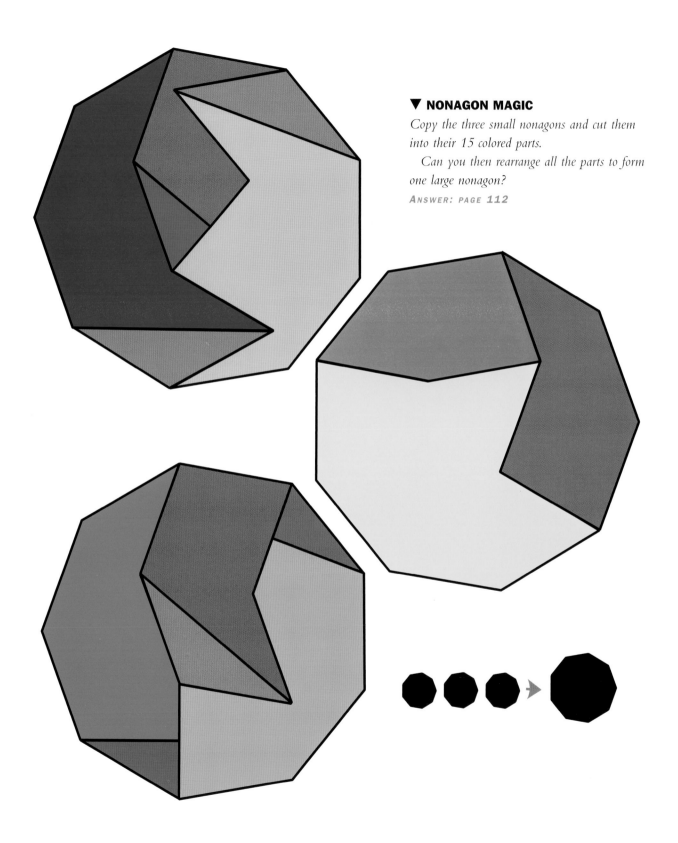

▼ NONAGON MAGIC

Copy the three small nonagons and cut them into their 15 colored parts.

Can you then rearrange all the parts to form one large nonagon?

ANSWER: PAGE *112*

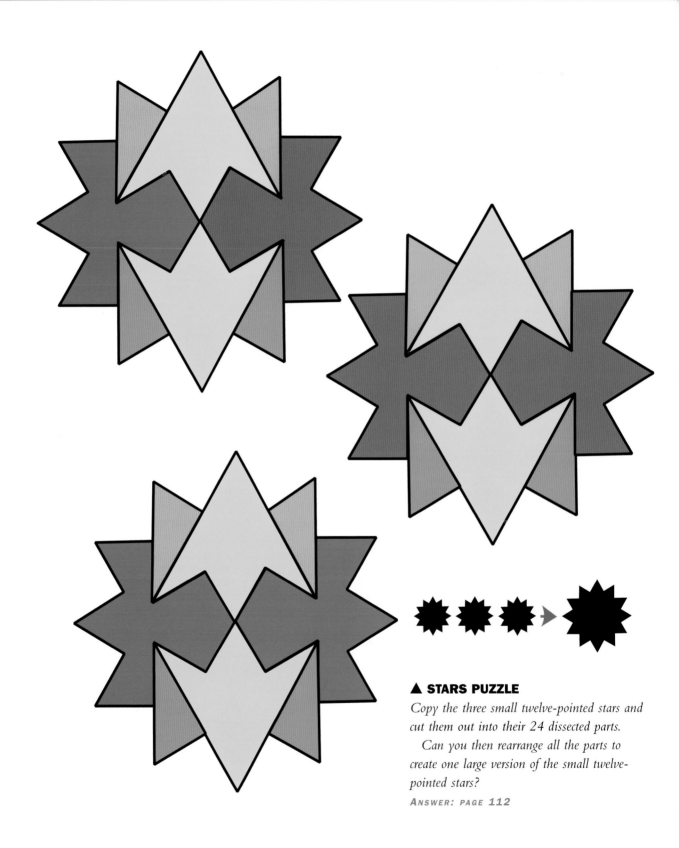

▲ STARS PUZZLE

Copy the three small twelve-pointed stars and cut them out into their 24 dissected parts.

Can you then rearrange all the parts to create one large version of the small twelve-pointed stars?

ANSWER: PAGE 112

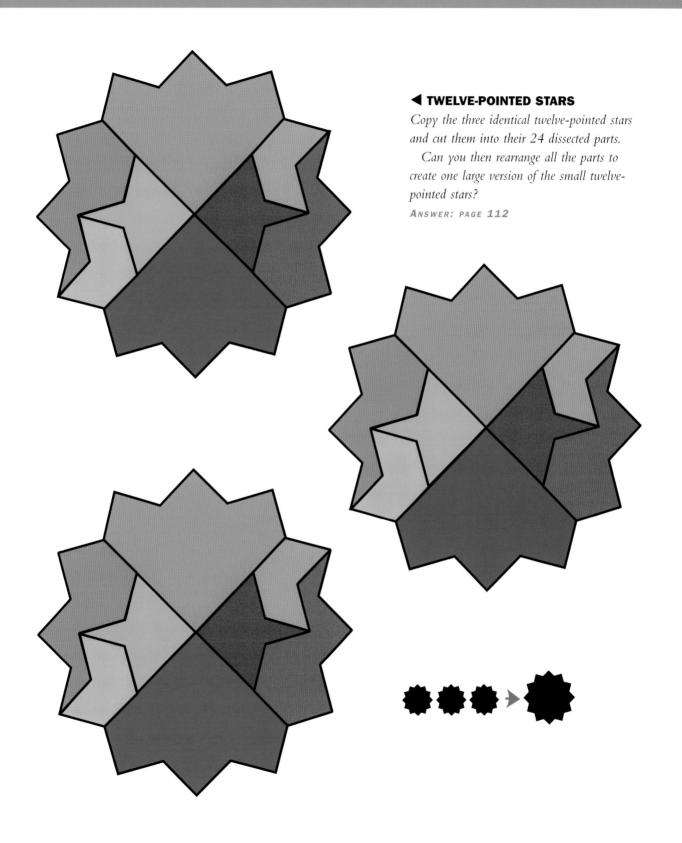

◀ TWELVE-POINTED STARS

Copy the three identical twelve-pointed stars and cut them into their 24 dissected parts.

Can you then rearrange all the parts to create one large version of the small twelve-pointed stars?

ANSWER: PAGE 112

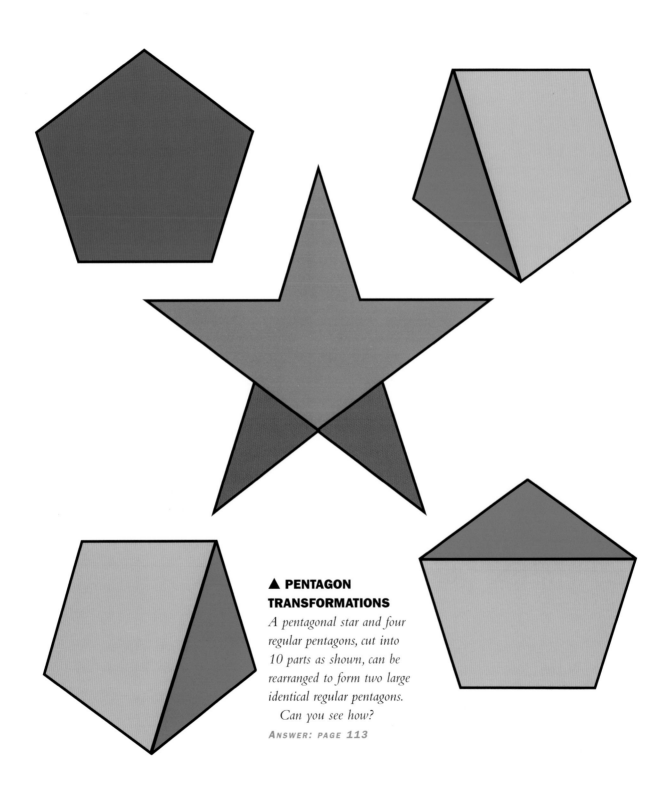

▲ PENTAGON TRANSFORMATIONS

A pentagonal star and four regular pentagons, cut into 10 parts as shown, can be rearranged to form two large identical regular pentagons.

Can you see how?

ANSWER: PAGE 113

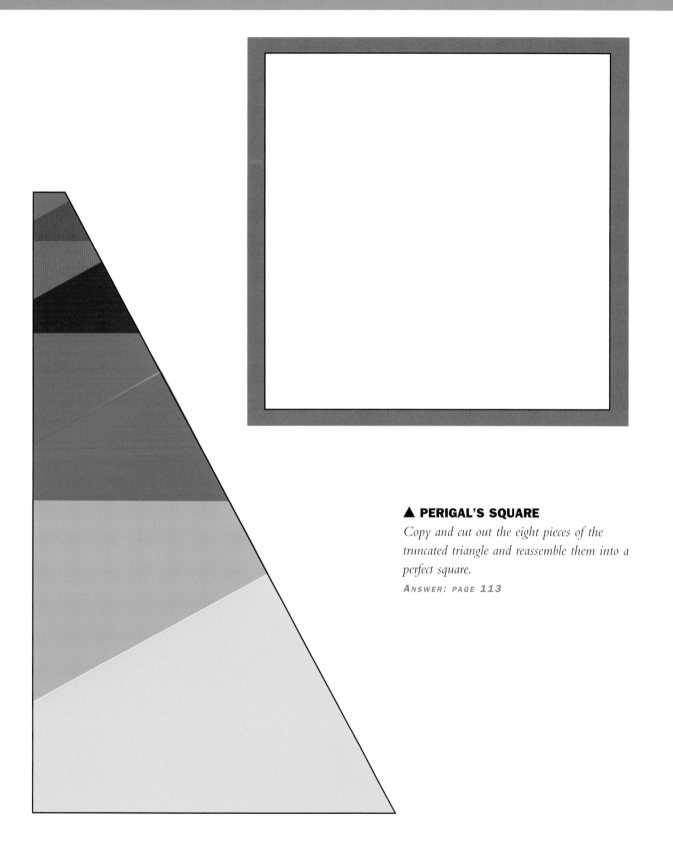

▲ PERIGAL'S SQUARE

Copy and cut out the eight pieces of the truncated triangle and reassemble them into a perfect square.

ANSWER: PAGE 113

Although he lived over two and a half millennia ago, Pythagoras's name lives on even for those with only a passing knowledge of mathematics. His theorem is probably one of the most famous ever.

✳ Pythagorean theorem

The ancient geometric theorem attributed to Pythagoras is one of the select few theorems that almost everybody has at least a nodding acquaintance with. It deals with the relationships between the two shorter sides of a right-angled triangle and the longer side (hypotenuse).

Because the Pythagorean theorem is so famous and important in mathematics, several hundreds of different ways to prove it have been discovered and published over the centuries. Leonardo da Vinci created an original proof and many other mathematicians are creating them still.

The theorem is:

The square on the hypotenuse is the sum of the squares on the other two sides.

In symbols:

$a^2 + b^2 = c^2$

where a and b are the lengths of the two shorter sides, and c is the length of the hypotenuse.

But what does this actually mean?

In numerical terms, it means that we may construct right-angled triangles by using any three lengths a, b, and c that satisfy the Pythagorean condition $a^2 + b^2 = c^2$.

For example

$3^2 + 4^2 = 9 + 16 = 25 = 5^2$

so a triangle with sides 3, 4, and 5 is necessarily a right-angled triangle. There are many such whole-number Pythagorean triplets.

Geometrically, the Pythagorean theorem asserts an equality of areas. The square whose side is the hypotenuse c has exactly the same area as the sum of two squares along the other two sides combined.

PYTHAGORAS (569 B.C.–475 B.C.)

Pythagoras was born on the island of Samos in Greece. Credited by many as being the first pure mathematician, he founded a cultlike group, "the Brotherhood of Pythagoreans," fanatically devoted to the study of mathematics. Their motto was "Numbers rule the universe."

Nothing remains of Pythagoras's written works. Details of Pythagoras's life are known only through other writers, some of which used original sources.

The beliefs held by Pythagoras were: (1) that at its deepest level, reality is mathematical in nature, (2) that philosophy can be used for spiritual purification, (3) that the soul can rise to union with the divine, (4) that certain symbols have a mystical significance, and (5) that all brothers of the order should observe strict loyalty and secrecy.

While little is known about Pythagoras, it is certain that his school made considerable contributions to mathematics. They were interested in the principles of mathematics, the concept of number, the concept of geometrical figures, and the abstract idea of mathematical proofs.

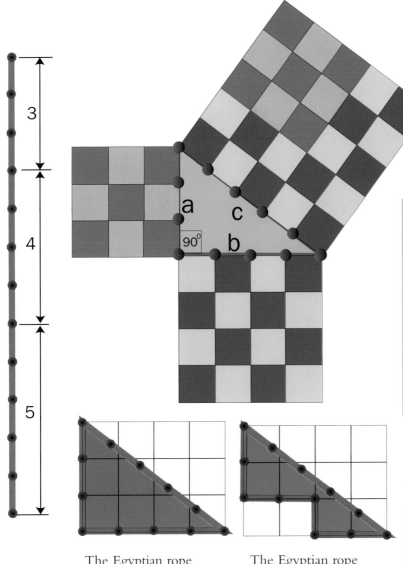

The Egyptian rope stretched into the Egyptian triangle of 6 units area.

The Egyptian rope stretched into a polygon of 4 units area.

✳ Egyptian triangle

The surveyors of ancient Egypt, it is said, used the simplest right-angled triangle to construct near-perfect right angles. To obtain it, they divided a rope into 12 equal parts by knots. They used such a rope to form a triangle whose sides are in the ratio 3 : 4 : 5.

This triangle is often called the Egyptian triangle, and is used to demonstrate the Pythagorean theorem in its simplest form. A visual proof of the Pythagorean theorem for the Egyptian triangle is shown.

◀ EGYPTIAN ROPE PUZZLES

As we have seen above, ancient Egyptian surveyors used a rope of 12 units length, divided into 12 equal parts by knots, to create triangles with an area of six units containing a right angle.

You can use a similar rope to create other shapes as well.

1) Can you form polygons that each have an area of four units using such a rope, stretching it to form polygons with straight edges?

One solution is shown. Can you find others?

2) What is the largest area which can be encompassed by the Egyptian rope held straight between points?

ANSWER: PAGE 114

Some problems seem impossible, but sometimes it's just the way you set about solving the problem. Often, computers pave the way for seeing things differently and will certainly create possibilities we have yet to even dream about.

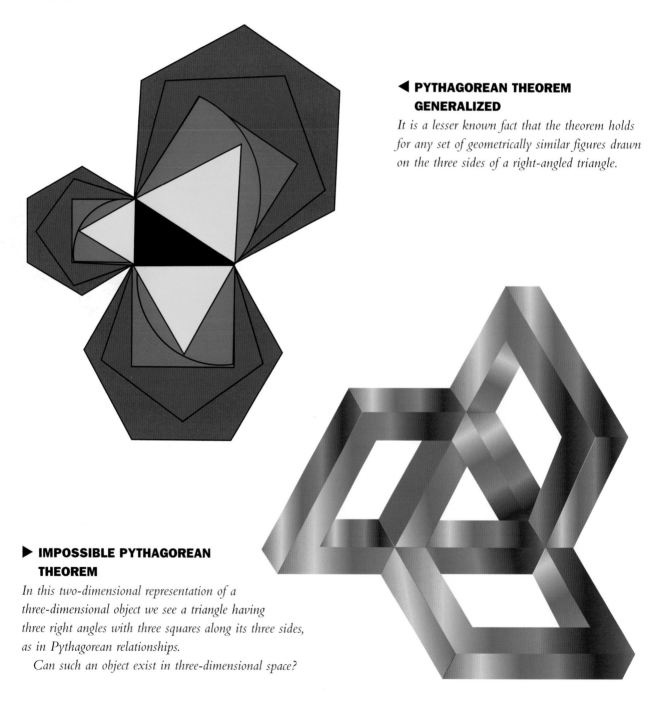

◄ PYTHAGOREAN THEOREM GENERALIZED

It is a lesser known fact that the theorem holds for any set of geometrically similar figures drawn on the three sides of a right-angled triangle.

▶ IMPOSSIBLE PYTHAGOREAN THEOREM

In this two-dimensional representation of a three-dimensional object we see a triangle having three right angles with three squares along its three sides, as in Pythagorean relationships.

Can such an object exist in three-dimensional space?

▶ DOG TIED

Fido is tied to a tree with a long rope. His leash reaches 10 yards from the tree.

His bone is 22 yards away from the point where Fido is standing. When he becomes hungry he can easily reach his bone.

How can this be?

ANSWER: PAGE 114

If you've watched enough science fiction movies you may be well acquainted with gravity-defying astronauts and even aliens. But did you know you can achieve a similar effect down here on Earth…?

✳ Center of gravity

You can't actually see the invisible point that is the center of gravity of every object but it's there. It is the point at which we can imagine the total weight of a body is concentrated and acts. In a simple sphere it is at the center. In other irregular bodies it can be anywhere, even outside of the object.

The center of gravity of an object tends to occupy, if possible, the lowest position in which unstable equilibrium becomes stable.

▲ ANTIGRAVITY CONES

Can an object defy gravity?

Galileo devised many ingenious mechanical experimental devices, among them the simple device shown in the illustration above.

Can you figure out what will happen when you place the double cone on the tracks at their lowest points at one of the ends and release it?

ANSWER: PAGE 114

ANTIGRAVITY RAILWAY
Here's a self-moving railway carriage concept. The fascinating behavior of the antigravity cones of Galileo inspired a Victorian inventor in 1829 to conceive the concept illustrated above based on the motion of the cones.

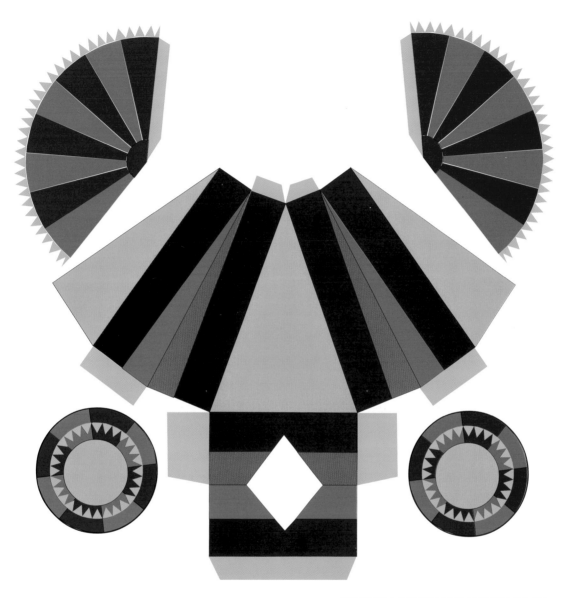

Above are do-it-yourself folding diagrams for building a working model of the antigravity cones. It is best made of stiff cardboard; you will need two copies of the track.

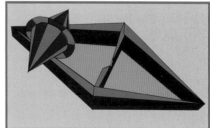

The antigravity cones

Perhaps the most intricate packing puzzle would be to piece together every single fragment of a broken window. However, the packing problems below are surely more fun (and less dangerous).

◄ PYTHAGOREAN SQUARE

Can you rearrange the 12 shapes to form a perfect square?

ANSWER: PAGE *115*

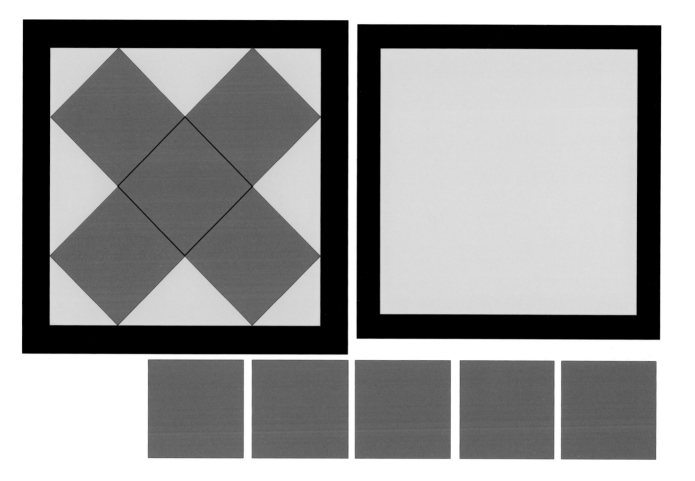

▲ PACKING FIVE SQUARES

Five unit squares are packed into a square, the side of which is 2.828 units.

Can you rearrange the 5 unit squares into the smaller square shown above?

ANSWER: PAGE 115

❋ Squares within squares

Suppose you have a number of identical squares to pack inside a larger square. What is the smallest size that the large box has to be to fit a given number of smaller squares without overlaps? If the smaller squares are not allowed to tilt, the problem is trivial. Allowing tilting adds to the difficulty, but it also allows more efficient solutions to emerge.

For n = 6, 7, 8, or 9, the untilted solutions are as efficient as any other. But when you must pack 10 and 11 squares, tilting provides better solutions, although no one yet knows if the solutions so far obtained are the best or whether some ingenious packing can improve upon them.

Strangely enough, for 12, 13, 14, and 15 squares, tilting, again, does not provide any advantage.

As the number of squares becomes large, the task of proving that a given packing is minimal becomes increasingly difficult, except in cases in which the number of squares is itself a square—that is, 9, 16, 25, and so on.

PACKING 11 UNIT SQUARES

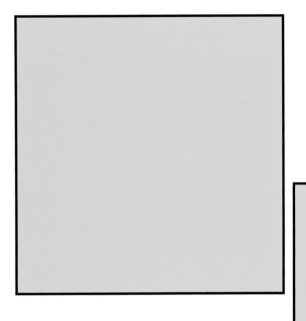

PACKING 17 UNIT SQUARES

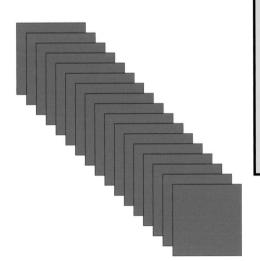

▲ PACKING UNIT SQUARES

Eleven, seventeen, and nineteen identical red unit squares have to be packed in the yellow square areas.

There are two rules:

1) Squares must stay within the yellow area.

2) No overlapping of the unit squares is allowed.

ANSWER: PAGE *116*

PACKING 19 UNIT SQUARES

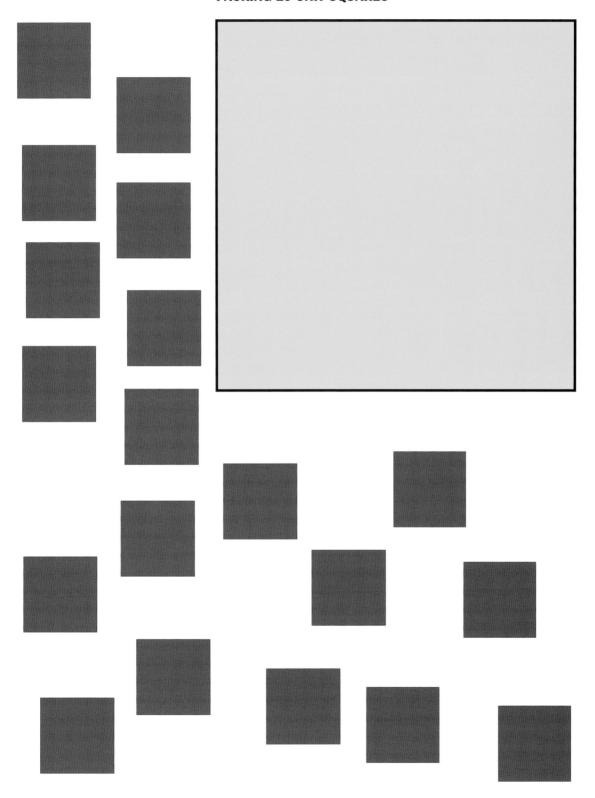

You're ready to go on vacation and then you remember one more thing you need to fit into the suitcase. Usually it's too big or awkward but you're adamant it'll make it in. This is a good frame of mind to try the following puzzles.

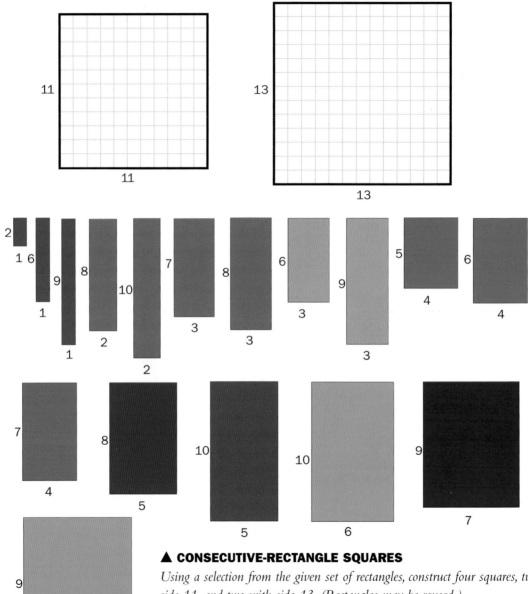

▲ CONSECUTIVE-RECTANGLE SQUARES

Using a selection from the given set of rectangles, construct four squares, two with side 11, and two with side 13. (Rectangles may be reused.)

Each of the four squares should consist of rectangles that have dimensions that use the numbers from 1 to 10 once each.

ANSWER: PAGE 116

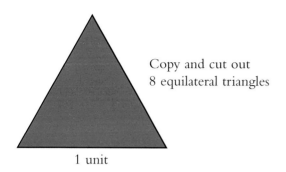

Copy and cut out
8 equilateral triangles

1 unit

▲ PACKING TRIANGLES IN SQUARES

Can you pack 5, 7, and 8 equilateral triangles of unit sides into the outlines of the given squares?

The solutions were found by the great puzzlist Erich Friedman, from the Math and CS Department of Stetson University.

ANSWER: PAGE 117

Puzzle 1: five equilateral triangles

Puzzle 2: seven equilateral triangles

Puzzle 3: eight equilateral triangles

The situation is this: you need to tile a floor but some inconsiderate person has only given you tiles of different sizes. What do you do? Make it into a puzzle, of course—home improvement has never been so much fun.

❋ Consecutive squares

So far we have seen problems involving packing identical squares. But what about packing non-identical squares?

One possibility that springs to mind is to use squares of side 1, 2, 3, 4 ... and so on, up to some particular limit. Can a large square be found which can be completely covered without overlap by such a sequence of smaller squares?

The consecutive squares problem is one of the gems of recreational geometry.

The first requirement for solving this problem is to add up the areas of the consecutive squares until the result is a square number.

But $1^2 + 2^2 = 5$

$1^2 + 2^2 + 3^2 = 14$

$1^2 + 2^2 + 3^2 + 4^2 = 30$

None of these are perfect squares. If we keep continuing the series, we find eventually that

$1^2 + 2^2 + 3^2 + 4^2 + ... 24^2 = 4,900 = 70^2$

In fact, this is not only the first, but the only way to add consecutive squares and obtain a square for the total. (The demonstration is a difficult exercise in number theory, and was itself an unsolved problem for a considerable time).

Given that the areas of the first 24 consecutive squares equal the area of a 70-by-70 square, this raises the following geometrical problem:

Is it possible to pack squares of sides 1, 2, 3, ... 24 into the 70-by-70 square?

Equality of areas is a necessary condition—but might not be sufficient. And, in fact, a complete packing is impossible.

The problem must therefore be rephrased: how many of the first 24 squares is it possible to pack into the 70 x 70 square? The best answer known to date is "all but one," and in every known example it is the 7 x 7 square that must be left out.

Twenty-four distinct solutions of this kind exist, but it is still not known if a better way of packing can be found, omitting squares totaling a smaller area than 7 x 7 = 49. To tackle this problem, cut out a set of 24 consecutive squares from stiff cardboard of sides from 1 to 24 centimeters. Now draw a 70 x 70 centimeter square and divide it into unit squares. Try to place as many of the cardboard squares as you can, without overlaps.

Another variation: given a set of consecutive squares, what is the smallest rectangle (in terms of total area) into which they will fit? Exhaustive enumeration of all possible arrangements would take far too long, even on a fast computer, for most such problems. Trial-and-error experiments can find solutions, if they exist; but to eliminate possibilities altogether requires more cunning trickery—in short, a mathematical insight.

All these problems can be made into competitive games. Players take turns placing squares within the boundary; the first player unable to move loses.

Here are two more questions about the set of 24 squares:

1) Can the odd-sided squares be fitted into a 48 x 48 square?

2) Can the even-sided squares be fitted into a 51 x 51 square?

23 squares in the 70 x 70 square

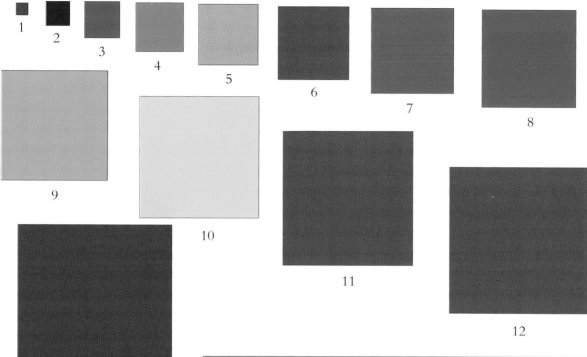

▲ SPIRALING CONSECUTIVE SQUARES

The first 13 consecutive squares are shown above.

In the picture, right, the first seven consecutive squares are spiraling around the central 1 x 1 square without leaving a hole.

How many more squares can be added in the same spiraling fashion around the center, covering the plane without leaving a hole?

ANSWER: PAGE 117

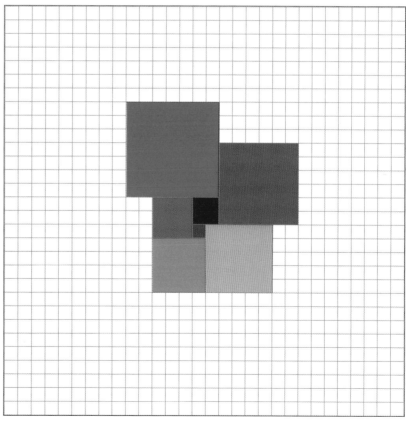

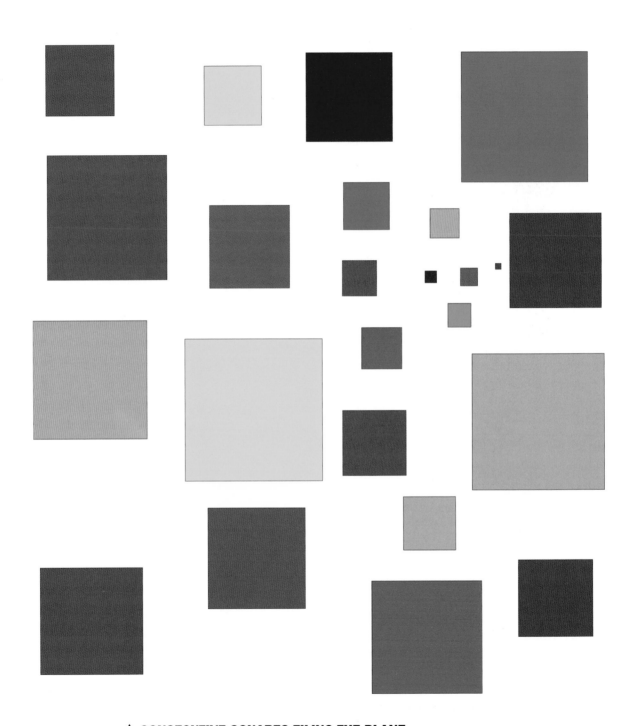

▲ CONSECUTIVE SQUARES TILING THE PLANE

Can you fit the first 24 consecutive squares within the outline of a 67-by-98 unit rectangle, forming a single connected shape with no internal holes?

ANSWER: PAGE 118

▲ DODECAGON FROM QUADRILATERALS

A dodecagon can be dissected into 12 identical quadrilaterals, which are each composed of an equilateral triangle and half a square.

Can you form a dodecagon using the 12 pieces?

ANSWER: PAGE *118*

SQUARES TO INFINITY

Is it possible to tile an infinite plane with squares, no two of which are of the same size?

Until the 1930s this problem was considered impossible. The closest solution had existed for ages, and can be seen at right. It involves the Fibonacci sequence (which frequently recurs in nature). By setting up a Fibonacci spiral of consecutive squares with sides of consecutive Fibonacci numbers (1, 1, 2, 3, 5, 8, 13, 21, 34, 55, 89, 144, 233, 377, 610…), we can cover as large an area as we wish.

The blue square which represents the 14th Fibonacci number is too big to fit on our page. The series spirals outward, going on and on, covering the plane to infinity.

There is just one problem: the spiral of whirling squares starts with two unit squares, which contradicts the condition that no two squares be the same size. But if we could solve the following problem, we would then have the solution to the infinite tiling problem:

Can a square to be subdivided into smaller squares, no two of which are alike?

This problem was only solved in 1938.

The first "Squared Square" or "Perfect Square" consisted of 55 squares, all different. Substituting that subdivided square into the first unit square of the spiraling Fibonacci squares solves the infinite tiling problem.

(Today the minimal perfect square consists of 21 squares of different sizes; it can be seen on the next page.)

Small is beautiful, as the saying goes. But is it perfection? Perhaps so when it's unique. Rather like the smallest perfect square puzzle, which truly is one of a kind.

✳ Perfect and imperfect squares and rectangles

The problem of squaring the circle goes back to the ancient Greeks, but that of squaring the square and rectangle is quite recent.

Mathematicians look for order everywhere. When they seem to discover it, they like to give expression to their enthusiasm by defining numbers, squares, rectangles, triangles, and parallelograms as "perfect," "imperfect," etc.

In 1934, Paul Erdös (1913–1996), the famous Hungarian mathematician, posed the following dissection problem:

Can a square or rectangle be subdivided into smaller squares, of which no two are alike?

Such squares or rectangles are called perfect, or squared.

Erdös wrongly concluded that such a square is impossible (probably influenced by the easily proven fact that one cannot dissect a cube into smaller cubes, no two of which are identical), and that the best one could achieve is to dissect a rectangle into smaller squares, no two of which are alike (see page 68).

For a long time it was not known whether any squared perfect squares existed. Eventually Roland Sprague found such a square. For years, it was believed that this square, requiring 55 squares (all different), was the smallest perfect square.

But in 1978, a better solution using a 112-by-112 square was found by A.J.W. Duijvestijn, a Dutch mathematician, requiring only 21 element squares. Presently, this is the smallest known squared square (or perfect square) and its pattern is unique (see page 67).

If some of the squares used in a dissection are allowed to be identical, the squares or rectangles are called "imperfect" (see page 72).

▼ SMALLEST PERFECT SQUARE

Here's a better look at the square on page 65, the lowest-order perfect square. It was discovered by A.J.W. Duijvestijn (1927–1998) and consists of 21 squares with sides measuring: 2, 4, 6, 7, 8, 9, 11, 15, 16, 17, 18, 19, 24, 25, 27, 29, 33, 35, 37, 42, and 50 units.

Now that you're proficient in the smallest perfect square, why not turn your attention to other shapes, like the rectangle?

▶ SMALLEST PERFECT RECTANGLE 1

Can a rectangle be subdivided into smaller squares no two of which are alike?

In 1909 Z. Moron discovered a rectangle dissectible into nine different squares, which, in 1940, Tutte, Brooks, Smith, and Stone proved to be the "smallest," meaning no smaller rectangle can be divided into nine different squares, and no rectangle at all can be divided into eight or fewer different squares.

The smallest perfect rectangle is composed of squares of sides 1, 4, 7, 8, 9, 10, 14, 15, and 18, as given here.

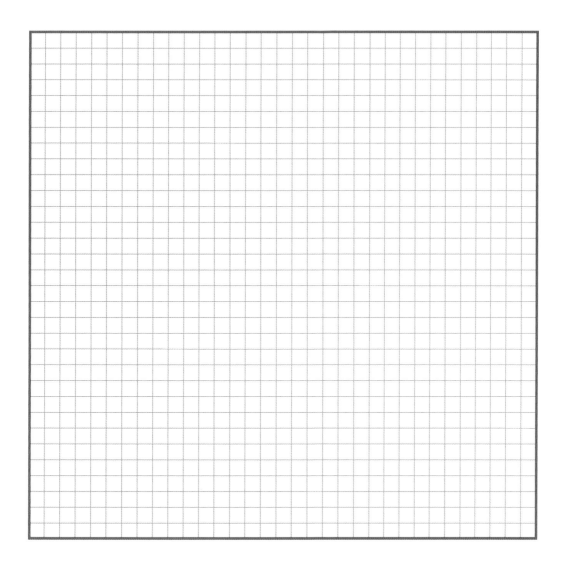

SMALLEST PERFECT RECTANGLE 1 (CONTINUED)

Can you use the nine squares (on the previous page) without overlap to form the smallest perfect rectangle of size 32 by 33?

There is exactly one other rectangle, of size 61-by-69, that can also be tiled by nine squares, of sides 2, 5, 7, 9, 16, 25, 28, 33, and 36 (see pages 70–71).

ANSWER: PAGE 119

2

5

7

9

16

25

28

33

36

▲ SMALLEST PERFECT RECTANGLE 2

Can you use these nine squares without overlap to form the second-smallest perfect rectangle?

ANSWER: PAGE 119

Being perfect isn't everything it's cracked up to be. Even imperfect squares have something to offer.

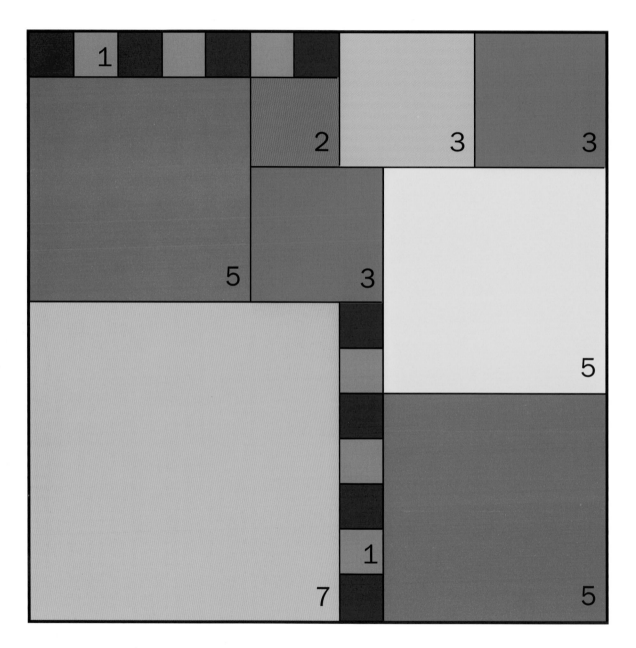

▲ IMPERFECT SQUARE SPLIT

Can you rearrange this 22-piece imperfect square into two smaller squares?

ANSWER: PAGE 119

▼ INCOMPARABLE RECTANGLES

In mathematics, two rectangles with sides of integral lengths are called incomparable if neither of them can fit inside the other (with their sides parallel).

The set of seven rectangles below are mutually incomparable, and can be packed into the smallest possible incomparably packed rectangle.

1) Can you determine the proportions of this rectangle that can be tiled by the set of seven incomparable rectangles?

2) Can you also find the pattern of the tiling?

The problem was posed by Edward Reingold in the American Mathematical Monthly, *in 1973.*

ANSWER: PAGE 120

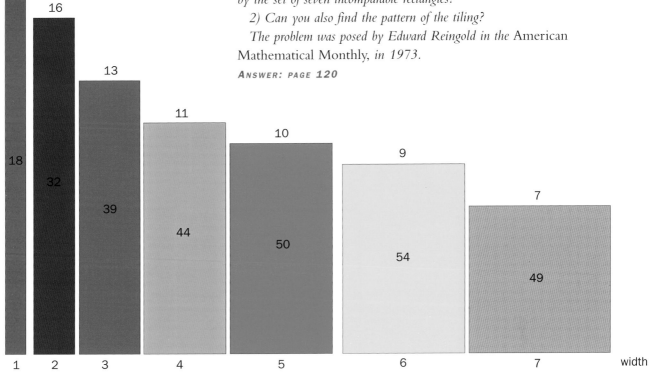

2) 4 squares

3) 8 squares

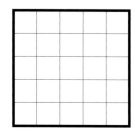

4) 4 squares

5

▲ MORE IMPERFECT SQUARES

Imperfect squares are squares packed with smaller squares along their unit grids. The squares are allowed to be identical. The problem is, what is the smallest number of squares with sides of integral lengths into which a square of side "n" can be split?

Grids of squares from 2 by 2 to 13 by 13 are shown.

Can you solve the minimal imperfect square packing for each?

To demonstrate the workings of the problem, a 2-by-2 square can only be divided into four small square units. A 3-by-3 square divides into one 2-by-2 square and five unit squares, a total of 6 pieces. The 4-by-4 square could be divided into one 3-by-3 square and seven unit squares, a total of eight pieces, but it can also be divided into four identical 2-by-2 squares, which is, of course, a better solution. In general, even values of "n" have a similar simple answer, but the problem is much subtler for odd squares, as you will find.

ANSWER: PAGE 121

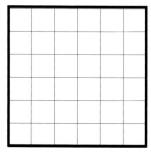

6

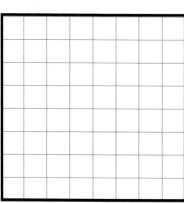

7

8

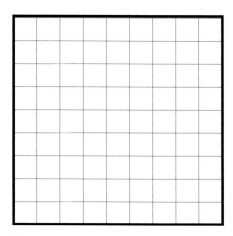

9

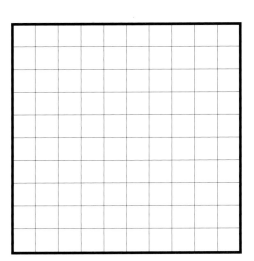

10

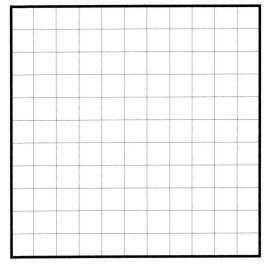

11

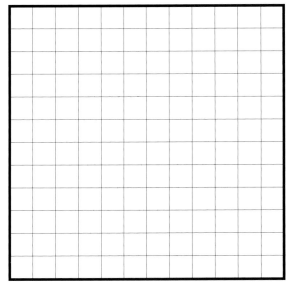

12

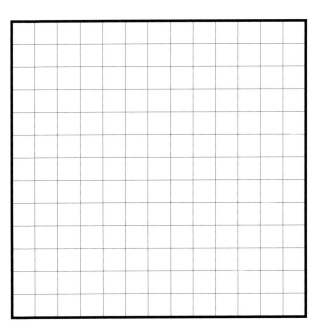

13

Here's a fine example of putting puzzles into practice. You've got 64 friends and each of them wants a piece of your chocolate bar. Quickly—how do you break it so everyone gets a piece with as little hassle as possible?

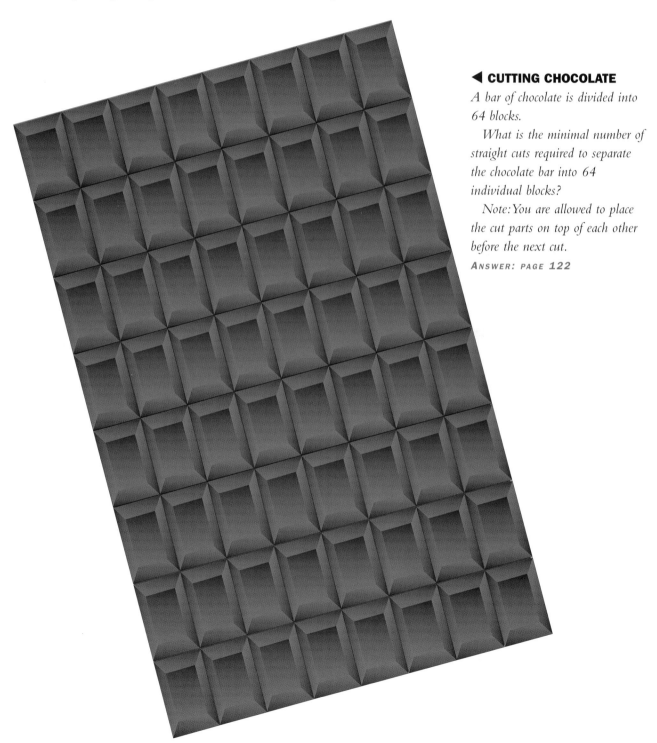

◀ CUTTING CHOCOLATE

A bar of chocolate is divided into 64 blocks.

What is the minimal number of straight cuts required to separate the chocolate bar into 64 individual blocks?

Note: You are allowed to place the cut parts on top of each other before the next cut.

ANSWER: PAGE 122

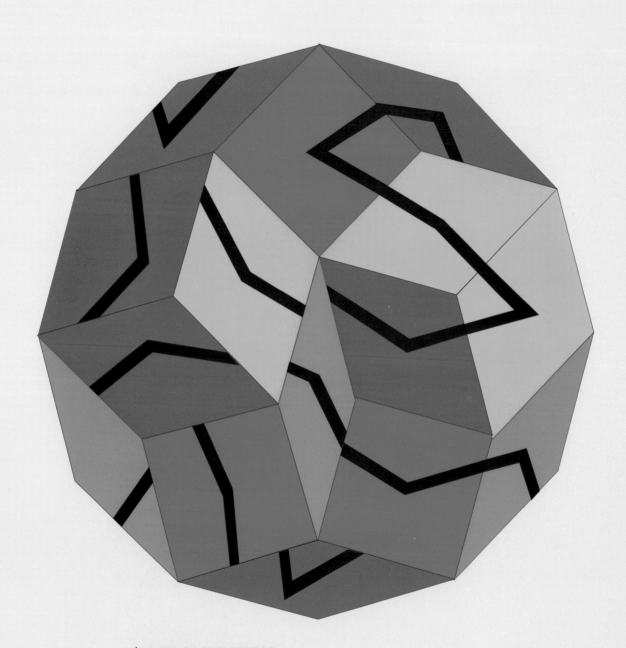

▲ DODECAGON ZIGZAG

Copy and cut out the 15 pieces forming the dodecagon. Rearrange the pieces to form a closed zig-zag line crossing all the pieces.

ANSWER: PAGE 122

You know the game … "In my suitcase I packed 11 rectangles, an imperfect hexagon, and a pair of trousers." Now it's your turn. Recite the contents of my bag and add one more to test me in return.

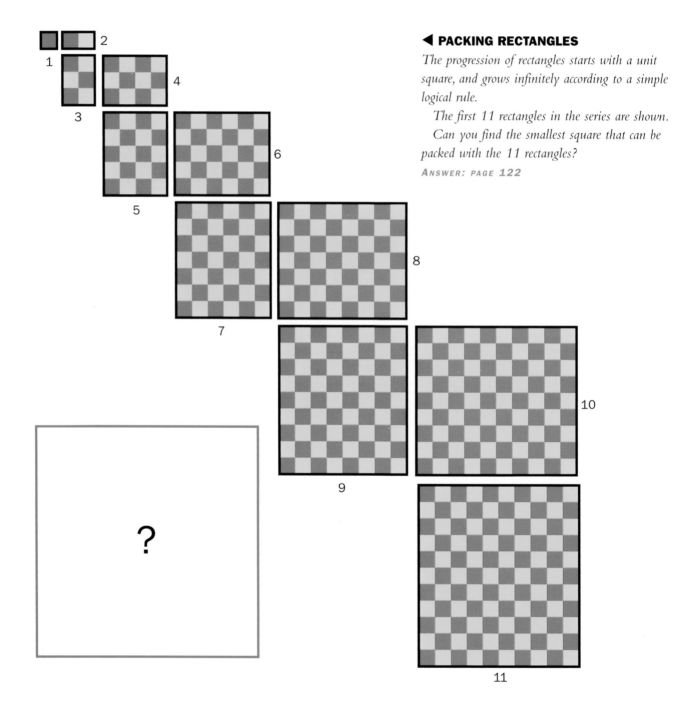

◀ PACKING RECTANGLES

The progression of rectangles starts with a unit square, and grows infinitely according to a simple logical rule.

The first 11 rectangles in the series are shown.

Can you find the smallest square that can be packed with the 11 rectangles?

ANSWER: PAGE 122

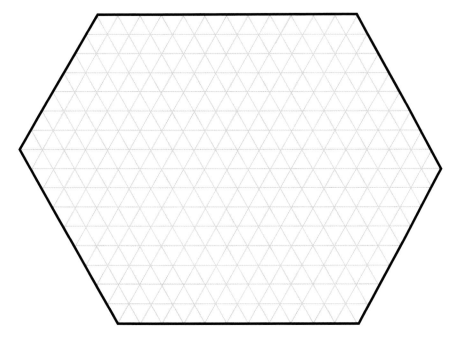

◀ IMPERFECT HEXAGON

Other polygons besides squares can be imperfect as well.

What is the smallest number of equilateral triangles that can cover the irregular hexagon grid shown at left?

Note that some of the triangles can be identical.

The same hexagon has been divided into 14 equilateral triangles without overlap.

Can you do better?

ANSWER: PAGE *123*

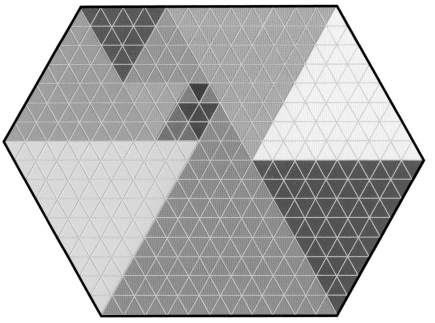

The third dimension—now there's height, width, and depth to contend with. Packing doesn't get any easier, unless of course you've got a personal butler to lend you a hand.

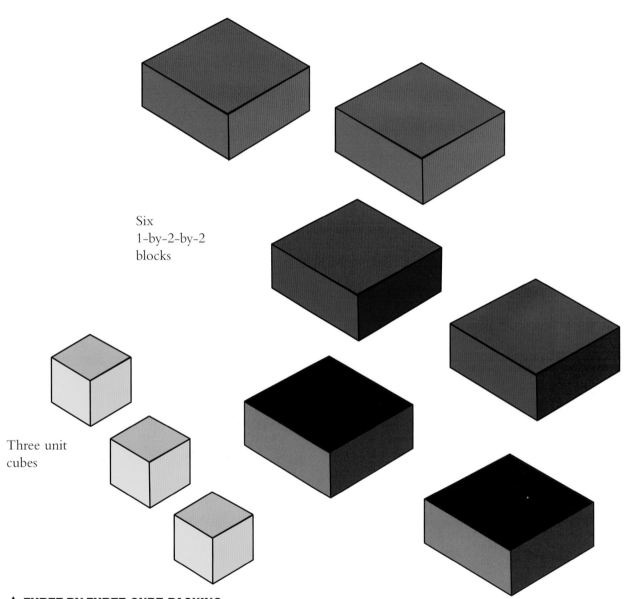

Six
1-by-2-by-2
blocks

Three unit
cubes

▲ THREE-BY-THREE CUBE PACKING

There are many three-dimensional packing puzzles in which sets of identical blocks have to be packed into given spaces.

One of the simplest 3-D packing problems involving non-identical blocks is seen above. The pieces are used to construct a 3-by-3 cube. It looks easy, but the solution can be frustratingly elusive and difficult to find.

It is a project that can easily be built out of cardboard or by gluing small cubes together. It is worth the effort, because the puzzle will certainly become a conversation piece.

ANSWER: PAGE **123**

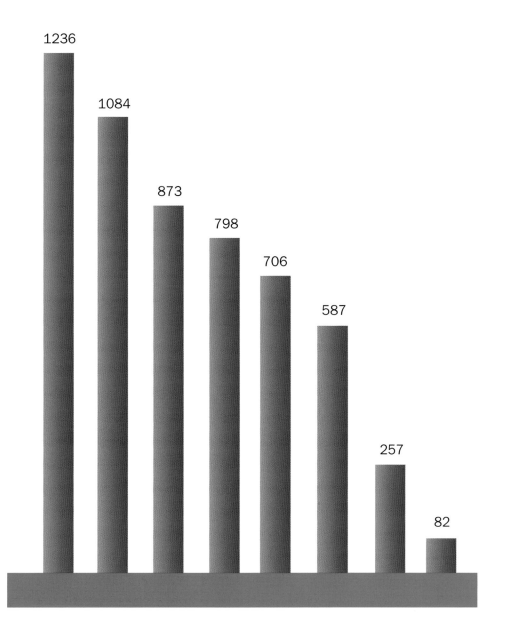

1236 1084 873 798 706 587 257 82 3154

▲ BOOKSHELF

This puzzle is a version of the so-called "bin-packing problem," in which we have a stock of planks in different lengths in millimeters, as shown, and the object is to select a number of shelves and join them to create a continuous length as near as possible to a certain specified length—in this case, 3154 mm—without cutting any of the given planks, if possible. How close to the target length can you get?

ANSWER: PAGE *123*

Clowning around never got anyone anywhere, or so they say. But along with some careful thought, it might help solve these problems.

◄ ROPE ACTS

The clown below is pulling the rope. What will happen to the nine acrobats hanging on the ropes? Which of them will go higher and which lower?

ANSWER: PAGE **124**

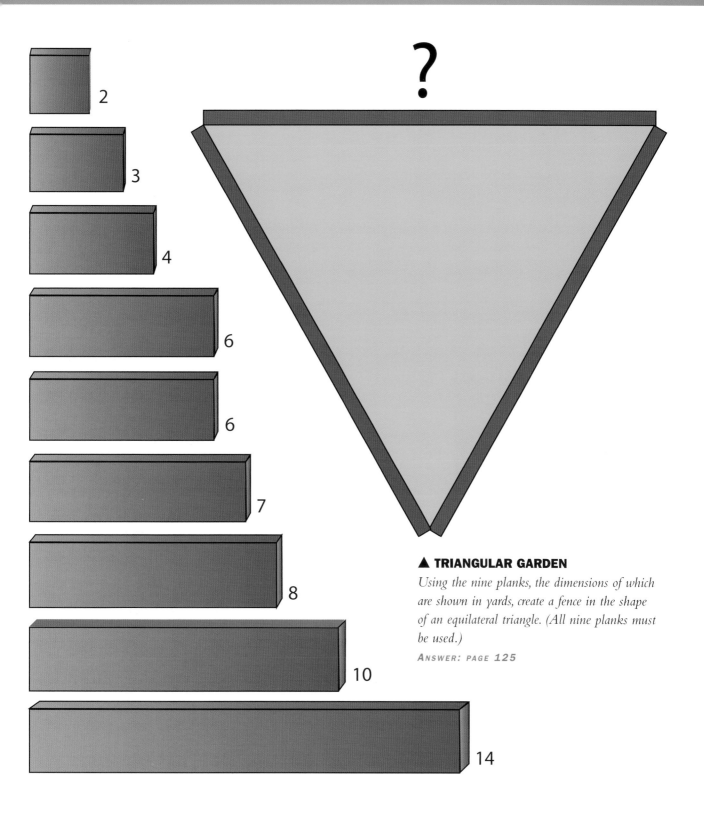

2

3

4

6

6

7

8

10

14

▲ **TRIANGULAR GARDEN**

Using the nine planks, the dimensions of which are shown in yards, create a fence in the shape of an equilateral triangle. (All nine planks must be used.)

ANSWER: PAGE *125*

Dealing with groups of items rather than individual objects can make puzzles much harder to solve. When there's a lot going on, it's easy to get distracted. See if you can focus on these two puzzles.

▼ STACKING WEIGHTS

Divide the groups of different weights shown in pounds into three stacks that are as close as possible in total weight.

With three weights of two pounds each and two weights of three pounds each, the solution would be easy. With nine weights, things are trickier. Can you manage it?

ANSWER: PAGE 125

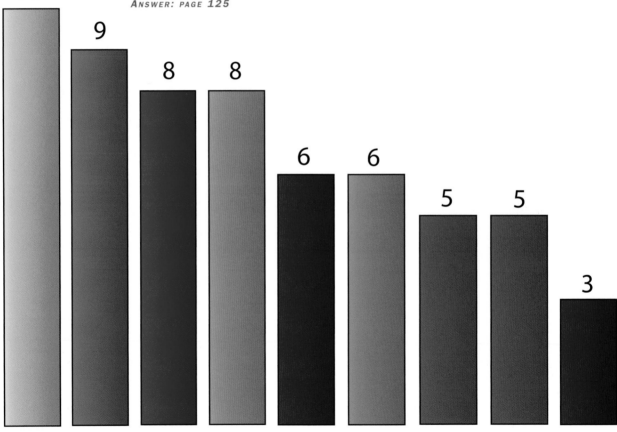

▲ DISAPPEARING FACE MAGIC

Copy the above illustration and cut it along the black line. Slide the lower strip one face to the left.

All the hats are still there, but one of the faces disappears.

Can you tell which face disappeared?

✳ Geometrical vanishes

Most optical tricks and perceptual illusions fail to hold our attention for too long because the secret of their trickery is generally obvious. But the remarkable group of images known as "geometrical paradoxes" or "geometrical vanishes" are so subtle that they continue to intrigue and surprise, becoming conversation pieces and causing us to question our sense of perception even after their workings have been explained.

Sam Loyd, the greatest American puzzle creator, was the originator of the most famous puzzle of this kind, the "Get Off the Earth" puzzle. Mel Stover and many others have perfected the art, creating subtle variations and perfections of the principle.

Geometrical paradoxes involve separating and rearranging parts of a total length or area. After rearrangement, a portion of the figure has somehow disappeared.

The explanation lies in the principle of concealed distribution, as Martin Gardner has named it, which depends on the eye's tolerance for the rearranged version. Often they fail to notice a tiny increase in the gaps between the parts or in the lengths of the reassembled pieces, and so believe both have the same length or area.

Apart from puzzles, the method of concealed distribution was once misused to make 15 $100 bills from only 14, by cutting each into two parts and gluing one part to the next. Please, don't try it!

Did you hear the joke about the disappearing pencil?
Actually, I won't bother telling it–there's no point!

THE DISAPPEARING PENCIL

Copy and cut out the disk in the upper left corner of the page.

If you superimpose the disk on the center of the lower diagram, and rotate it three spaces clockwise, you can change the diagram from having seven blue and six red pencils to six blue and seven red pencils.

Can you tell which pencil changed its color? This is one of Mel Stover's great variations on the classic vanish puzzle.

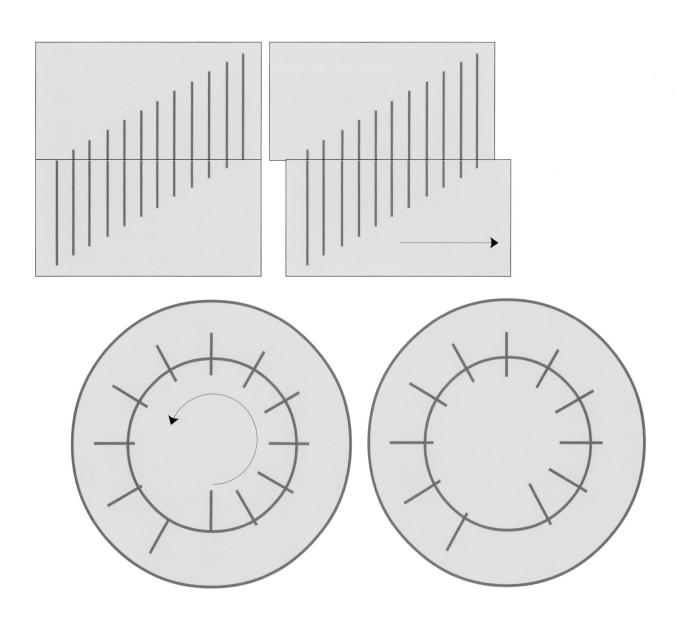

▲ GEOMETRICAL VANISHES EXPLAINED

Top: 12 vertical lines become 11 when the bottom half is shifted to the right.

Bottom: 12 radial lines become 11 when the inner wheels rotate one notch counterclockwise.

Obviously, in both cases nothing has really disappeared. The patterns were only rearranged, convincingly demonstrating the most elementary principle in geometry that the whole is equal to the sum of its parts, no matter how the parts are rearranged.

The two examples serve to explain the principle of concealed distribution, which is behind many seemingly magical vanishing tricks and paradoxes.

Ever have that feeling that no matter how many times you've counted something, there's always one missing? It could be a clever vanishing trick or maybe the sock has just slipped down the back of the drawer.

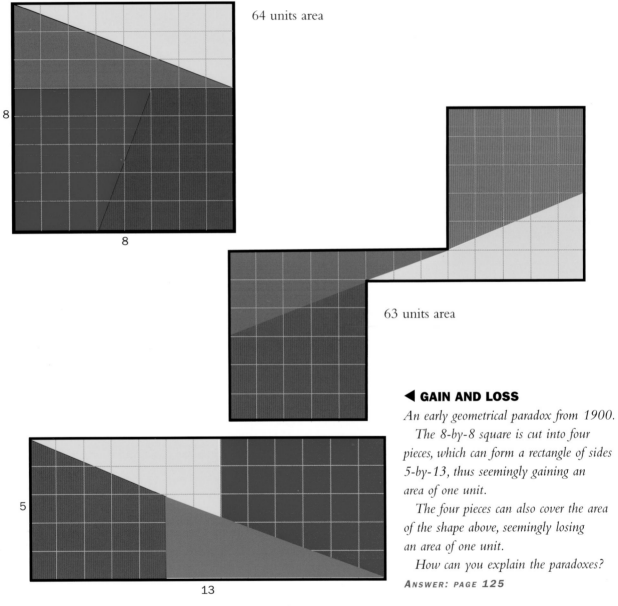

64 units area

8

8

63 units area

5

13

65 units area

◄ GAIN AND LOSS

An early geometrical paradox from 1900.

The 8-by-8 square is cut into four pieces, which can form a rectangle of sides 5-by-13, thus seemingly gaining an area of one unit.

The four pieces can also cover the area of the shape above, seemingly losing an area of one unit.

How can you explain the paradoxes?

ANSWER: PAGE **125**

▲ SPARE THE RECTANGLE

Copy and cut out the above diagram into five pieces. Rearrange the red and green pieces into a rectangle without using the small blue rectangle.

ANSWER: PAGE 125

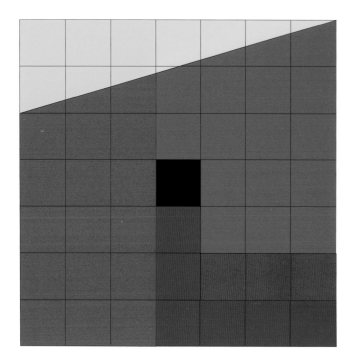

◄ CURRY'S PARADOX

Cut the square into six pieces as shown. Take away the small black square and rearrange the rest into the same square outline to cover it completely.

ANSWER: PAGE *126*

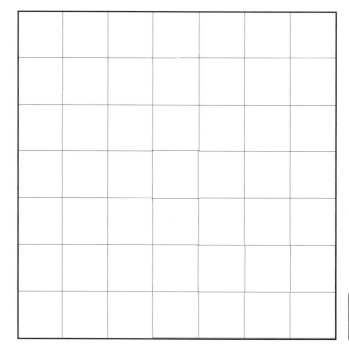

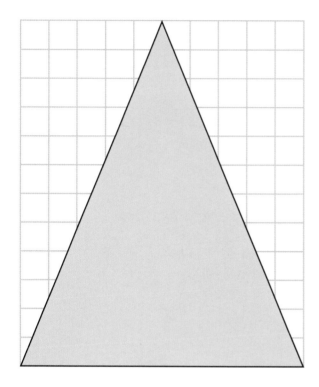

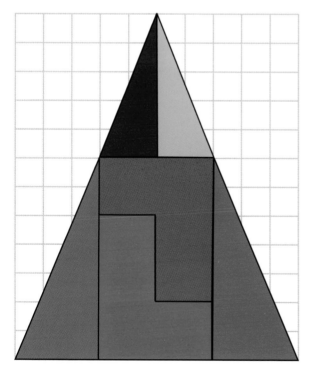

▲ CURRY'S TRIANGLE PARADOX

*The gray triangle has an area of 60
unit squares.*

*The six pieces also have a total area of
60 unit squares and they can cover the
triangle as shown.*

*Can you rearrange the pieces, again covering
the gray triangle, but with a big hole in the
middle left uncovered?*

ANSWER: PAGE **126**

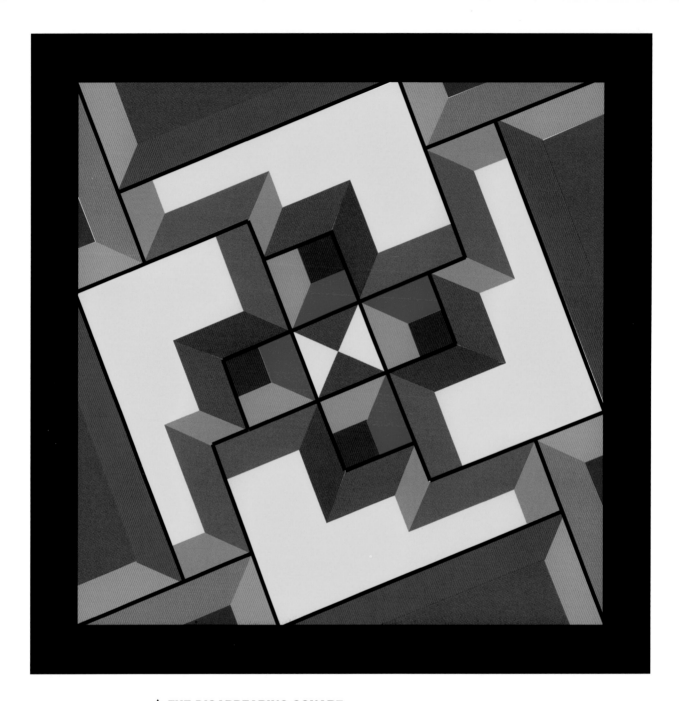

▲ THE DISAPPEARING SQUARE

Copy and cut out the 17 parts along the black lines.

Puzzle 1: *After you fit all the pieces into the square black outline, opposite, dismantle the puzzle and discard the small green-and-yellow square.*

ANSWER: PAGE 126

Puzzle 2: *Rearrange the remaining pieces in the same black square outline so that they re-form the initial square.*

It sounds impossible—but it isn't.

Where does the space for the small square go to?

ANSWER: PAGE 126

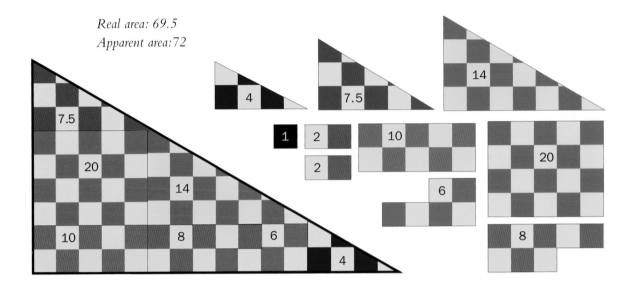

Real area: 69.5
Apparent area: 72

▶ TRIANGLE PARADOXES

Using subsets of the 10 shapes shown above right, one can assemble approximations of a 9-by-16 triangle (which would have a total area of 72 units) in six different ways, according to the six possible arrangements of the three triangles along the hypotenuse of the big triangle.

The areas of the six assembled triangles, some of them bigger than the area of the big triangle, some of them smaller, are nearly indistinguishable from the shape of the big triangle.

The first assembled triangle has an area of 69.5 units. Can you assemble the other 5 triangles with the real areas as shown?

The ingenious set of paradoxes based on Curry's paradox was created by Jean Brette, who was for many years in charge of the mathematics exhibits in the Palais de la Decouverte, the famous science museum in Paris, and was first published in the Mathematical Intelligencer *in 1991.*

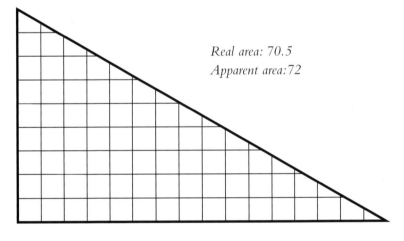

Real area: 70.5
Apparent area: 72

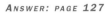

ANSWER: PAGE 127

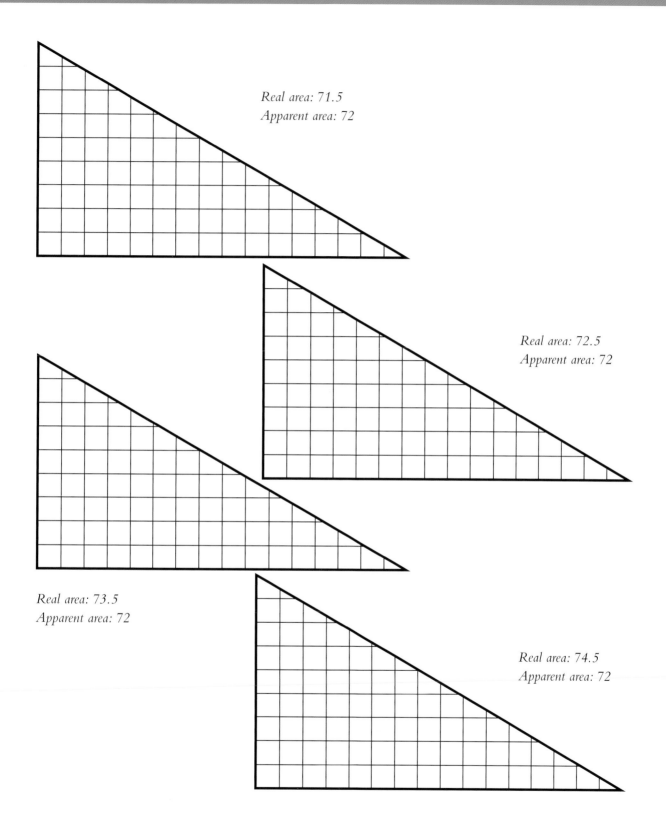

Real area: 71.5
Apparent area: 72

Real area: 72.5
Apparent area: 72

Real area: 73.5
Apparent area: 72

Real area: 74.5
Apparent area: 72

345   543 – 345 = ?
456   654 – 456 = ?
567   765 – 567 = ?
678   876 – 678 = ?
789   987 – 789 = ?
1234   4321 – 1234 = ?
2345   5432 – 2345 = ?
3456   6543 – 3456 = ?
4567   7654 – 4567 = ?
5678   8765 – 5678 = ?
6789   9876 – 6789 = ?

▲ CONSECUTIVE UNIQUE NUMBERS

Puzzle 1: *How many 2-digit numbers are there, excluding 2-digit numbers with consecutive digits?*

Puzzle 2: *How many 2-digit numbers are there, excluding 2-digit numbers with identical digits?*

Puzzle 3: *Take a number with 3 consecutive digits, for example, 234. If subtracted from its reverse (432) you get 198. This is true for all such three-digit numbers.*

How long will it take you to follow a similar procedure with the above list of 4-digit numbers and tabulate the results?

Can you do it in less than a minute?

ANSWER: PAGE 128

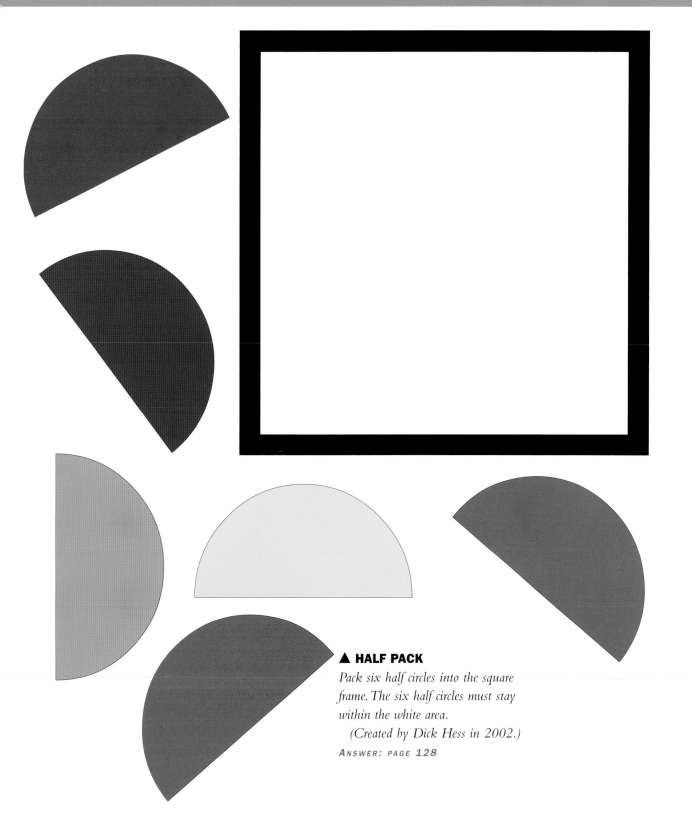

▲ HALF PACK

Pack six half circles into the square frame. The six half circles must stay within the white area.

(Created by Dick Hess in 2002.)

ANSWER: PAGE 128

▼ DISSECTING SPACE (page 8)

15 parts.

The parts are the following:

Four at the vertices.

Six at the edges.

Four at the faces of the tetrahedron.

The tetrahedron itself.

The total is 15 regions.

This number is the maximum number of regions into which three-dimensional space can be divided with four plane cuts.

▼ CONSECUTIVE WATERMELONS (page 10)

? ? ? 7 ? ? ?

1 3 5 7 9 11 13

The heaviest melon is 13 kg.

▼ FALLING BRICK (page 10)

Did the question confuse you?

Many think the answer is 1.5 kilograms, when it is really 2 kilograms.

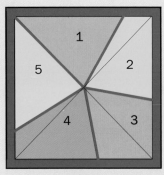

▼ SQUARE CAKE (page 9)

All you need to do is to mark the perimeter in 5 (or "n," where n is the number of slices you need) equal lengths and cut the cake from the center in the usual manner.

Norman Nelson and Forest Fisch provided the proof in 1973, demonstrated visually below.

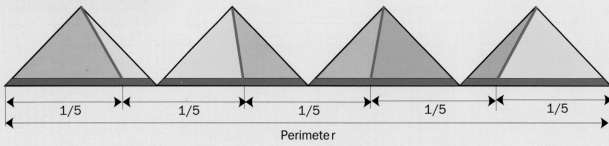

| 1/5 | 1/5 | 1/5 | 1/5 | 1/5 |

Perimeter

▼ T-TIME (page 11)

▼ TANGRAM (page 12)

▶ **TANGRAM NUMBERS (page 13)**

▶ **TANGRAM POLYGONS (page 14)**

The set of 13 tangram convex polygons.

▼ TANGRAM POLYGONS PACKING GAME 1
(page 15)

11-by-11 square

▼ TANGRAM POLYGONS PACKING GAME 2
(page 15)

11-by-12 square

▼ TANGRAM PARADOXES (page 16)

▼ **TRIANGLE TANGRAM (page 17)**

▼ **CHESSBOARD DISSECTION (page 18)**

▼ **PENTAGONAL STAR (page 19)**

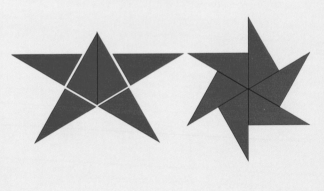

▼ **HEART TANGRAM** (page 20)

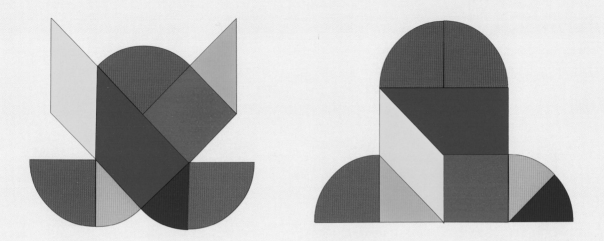

▼ **CIRCLE TANGRAM** (page 21)

▼ DIAGONAL CROSSING (page 22)

23 squares are crossed in the 10-by-14 rectangle.

Can we conclude that the general formula for the number of squares crossed by the diagonals is:

The sum of the two sides of the rectangles − 1?

Will this work with every rectangle?

Try the 9-by-6 rectangle.

We get 9 + 6 − 1 = 14, but when we count the number of squares crossed we can see it is only 12. Obviously our formula doesn't work when the diagonal crosses corners of squares. The diagonals will cross at least one corner if the shape is a square, or if the length of the rectangles' sides share common factors. For example, 9 and 6 share a common factor of 3.

Our formula will work for both even and odd rectangles if you count each of intersection at a corner as an additional square crossed.

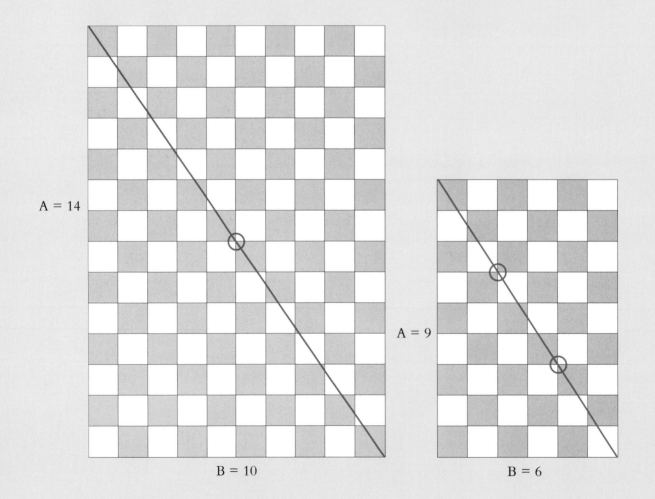

A = 14

B = 10

A = 9

B = 6

▼ SQUARE DISSECTIONS (page 23)

The 27 ways to dissect a square into six similar right-angled isosceles triangles.

▼ CHRISTMAS MOBILE (page 24)

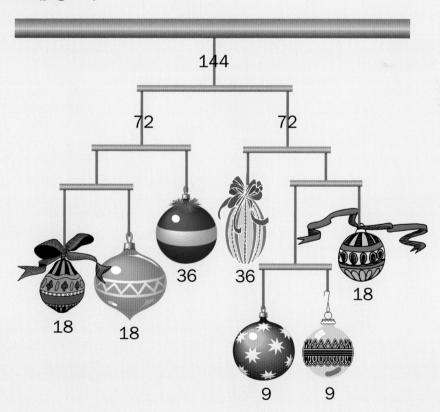

▼ FORCE FOUR (page 25)

Addition of Vectors

The resultant of several forces can be obtained by taking two forces and creating their resultants in sequence until you obtain the final resultant, or adding the forces together as shown.

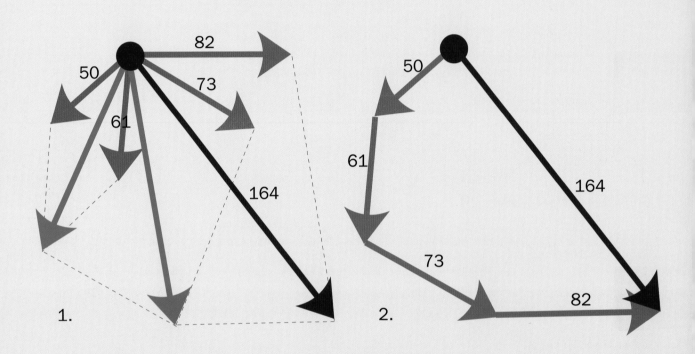

1.

2.

▼ THREE WEIGHTS (page 26)

There are six possible ways to arrange the three identical boxes.

A single weighing can decide between two possibilities, two weighings among four possibilities, three weighings among eight, and so on.

In general, "n" weighings will determine 2^n possibilities at most.

In our case, say we have:

Weighing 1: A > B

Weighing 2: A < C

Conclusion: C > A > B, and the problem is solved.

If weighing 2: A > C

There may then be two possibilities:

A > B > C

or A > C > B

and a third weighing will be needed to compare B and C. So a maximum of 3 weighings is required.

▼ TRIOMINO DISSECTING (page 27)

It is obvious that the L-triomino can be dissected into any multiple of n = 3. The solution for n = 4 is a classic puzzle in which the dissected parts are of the same shape as the original triomino (such shapes are called reptiles). Since each of these reptiles can be further dissected into four parts, solutions exist for any n that is a power of 4 (16, 64, etc.)

The solution shape for n = 2 is another reptile, providing solutions for n = 8, 32, 128, 512…). Can you see how to dissect each half into 4 parts that are the same shapes as itself?

The problem was first described in the *Journal of Recreational Mathematics*, 1990.

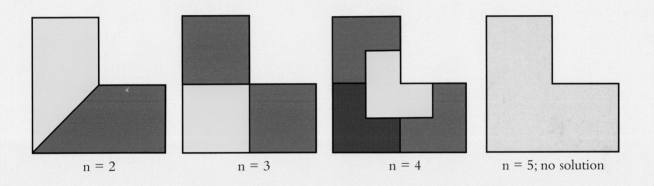

n = 2   n = 3   n = 4   n = 5; no solution

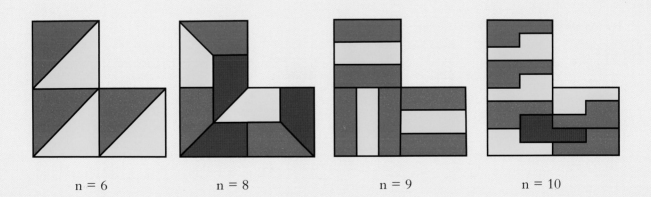

n = 6   n = 8   n = 9   n = 10

▶ **QUARTERING SQUARES**
(page 28)

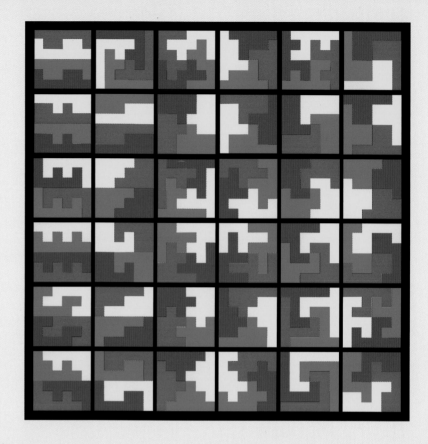

▶ **BOMB DEMOLITION EXPERT (page 29)**
Congratulations! Since you are still alive to check the answer, you must have done it with eight cuts as shown.

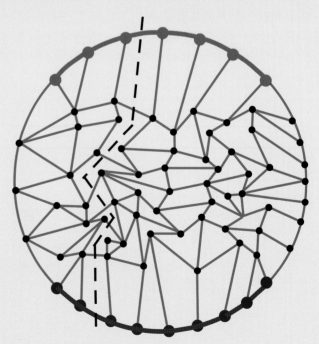

▼ QUARTERING SQUARES GAME (page 30)

This is my best effort. Can you do better?

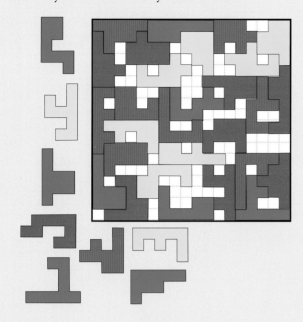

▼ POLYGONS FROM RHOMBUSES (page 33)

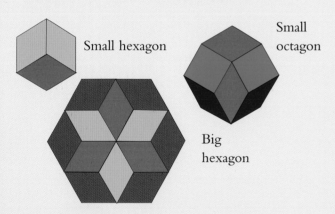

Small hexagon

Small octagon

Big hexagon

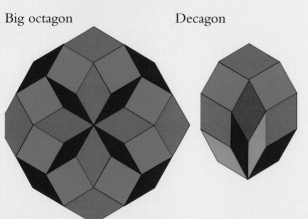

Big octagon

Decagon

▼ DODECAGONS FROM RHOMBUSES (page 32)

One of many possible answers.

▼ HEXAGON DISSECTION (page 34)

▼ TWENTY-ONE WEIGHTS (page 35)

Three weighings will be needed at the most.

1) Divide the 21 boxes into three groups of seven. Put one group on each side of the scale. There are two possible outcomess:

a) scales balance

b) scales tilt

If the two scales balance, the group containing the heavier box is the unweighed set. If the scales tilt, obviously the heavier side of the scale holds the group with the heavier box. Take the heavy group, divide it into two groups of three boxes with one box left over, and put one group of three on each side of the scale.

2) Again, there are two possible outcomes

a) scales balance

b) scales tilt

If the scales balance, the unweighed box is the heavier one, and no more weighings are needed. Otherwise, one more weighing will be needed, by putting one box on each side of the scale, with one left over.

▼ CANNON DROP AND FIRE (page 36)

The cannonball dropped and the one fired horizontally will hit the ground at the same time because objects fall vertically due to gravity at the same rate, regardless of their horizontal velocity. If the other two cannonballs have been launched with the same amount of energy, the one fired at an angle will hit the ground before the ball fired straight up. This is because some of the energy of the angled ball has been converted into horizontal motion, so it will not reach as high, and therefore its time of flight will be less.

▼ GRAVITY FALL (page 37)

Assuming no friction from air resistance, the heavy ball would drop with increasing speed until reaching Earth's center. At that point it would begin to slow until it reached the other side, when it would stop and begin falling again ad infinitum.

▼ SQUARE TO STAR (page 38)

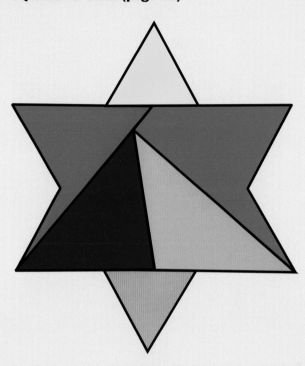

▼ HEXAGON TO TRIANGLE (page 39)

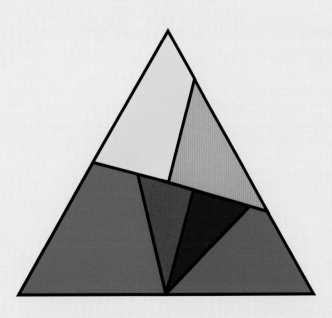

▼ PENTAGONAL STAR (page 40)

▼ **EXPLODING STAR (page 41)**

▼ **HEPTAGONAL STARS (page 42)**

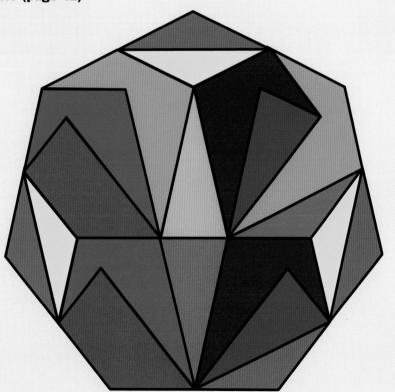

▼ **NONAGON MAGIC (page 43)**

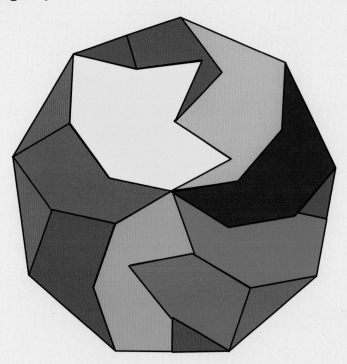

▼ **STARS PUZZLE (page 44)**

▼ **TWELVE-POINTED STARS (page 45)**

▼ **PENTAGON TRANSFORMATIONS (page 46)**

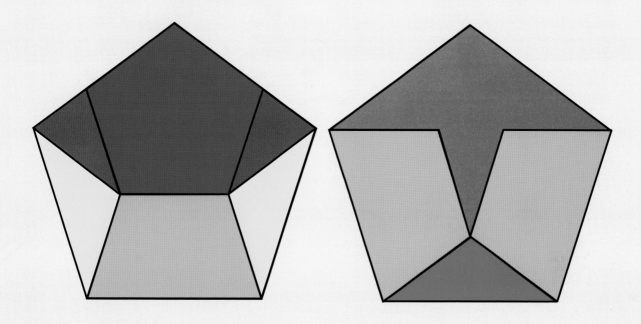

▼ **PERIGAL'S SQUARE (page 47)**

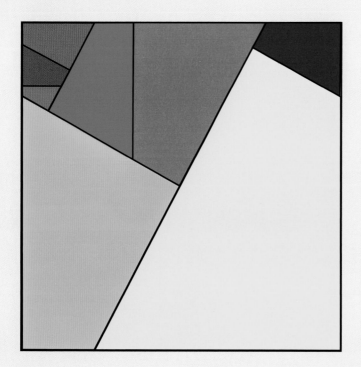

▶ EGYPTIAN ROPE PUZZLES (page 49)

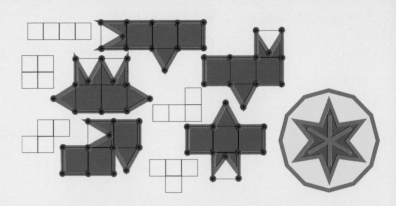

1) There are a large number of different four-unit area polygons that can be made with the Egyptian rope.

Elton Palmer, from Oakmont, Pennsylvania, ingeniously correlated this problem with polyominoes, specifically to tetrominoes. Each of the five tetrominoes can be the basis for a large number of solutions, simply by adding and subtracting triangles to accommodate the twelve equal lengths. Some solutions are shown using the five different tetrominoes.

2) Eugene Putzer, Charles Shapiro, and Hugh Metz suggested a star configuration solution as shown.

By adjusting the width of the star points, any area from 0 to 11.196 can be encompassed by the Egyptian rope. The largest area is that of a regular dodecagon.

▼ DOG TIED (page 51)

Fido is tied around a very thick tree with a diameter of over two yards. So by going around the tree Fido can cover a circular area with a diameter of 22 yards, as shown.

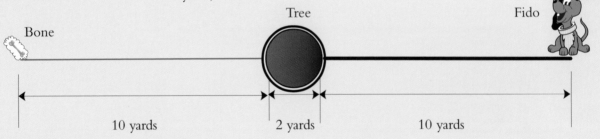

Bone

Tree

Fido

| 10 yards | 2 yards | 10 yards |

▶ ANTI-GRAVITY CONES (page 52)

The double cone will seemingly start going uphill, when it actually descends on the inclined track, as can be seen when the device is viewed from the side. As the double cone seemingly moves "up," the increasing width of the tracks lowers the cone so that in fact its center of gravity moves down.

On the inclined double tracks the motion of the double cone is that of a mechanical oscillator, with its center of gravity going up and

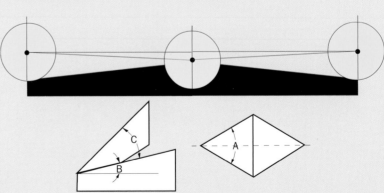

down, to and fro; this oscillation may go on for a long time if the cones are heavy.

▶ PYTHAGOREAN SQUARE (page 54)

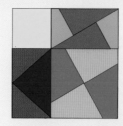

▶ PACKING FIVE SQUARES (page 55)

The five unit squares packed into a square of the smallest area, with a side of 2.707 units.

Here are the best known results for packing "n" unit squares into the smallest square, when "n" ranges from n = 1 to n = 10; "k" is the length of the square's side.

n = 1; k = 1   n = 2; k = 2   n = 3; k = 2   n = 4; k = 2

n = 5; k = 2.707   n = 6; k = 3   n = 7; k = 3

    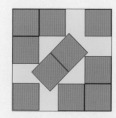 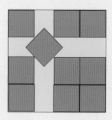

n = 8; k = 3   n = 9; k = 3   n = 10; k = 3.707   n = 10; k = 3.707

▼ PACKING UNIT SQUARES (page 56)

PACKING 11 SQUARES

The side of the square is 3.877+ units. The tilted squares are at 40.18 degree angles.

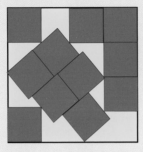

PACKING 17 SQUARES (page 56)

The 17 unit squares are packed in a square measuring 4.707+ units per side.

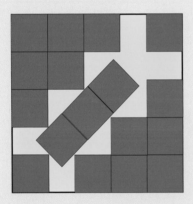

PACKING 19 SQUARES (page 57)

This packing solution was discovered by Robert Wainwright and several others.

The side of the square is 4.885+ units.

▼ CONSECUTIVE-RECTANGLE SQUARES (page 58)

If the first ten positive integers are the dimensions of five rectangles that can be assembled into a square, the area of the square must lie between 110 and 190.

Consequently, the side of the square may be 11, 12, or 13.

Since the 10 dimensions of the rectangles are distinct, four rectangles must be surrounding a central rectangle.

There is no solution for a square of side 12. There exist only four solutions: two of side 11, and two of side 13. These are the solutions of our puzzle, shown below.

The problem was first published by Charles Trigg in the *Journal of Recreational Mathematics* in 1969.

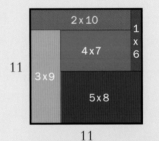

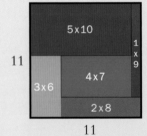

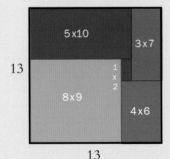

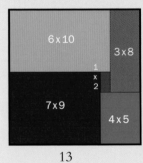

▼ PACKING TRIANGLES IN SQUARES (page 59)

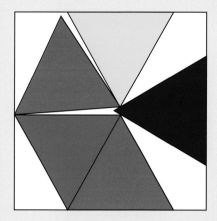 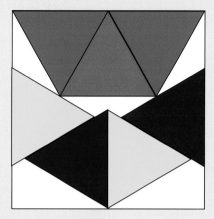 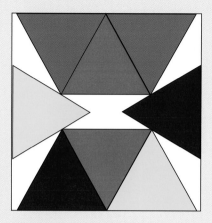

Puzzle 1: 5 equilateral triangles
Side of smallest square: 1.803+ units

Puzzle 2: 7 equilateral triangles
Side of smallest square: 2 units

Puzzle 3: 8 equilateral triangles
Side of smallest square: 2.098+ units

▶ SPIRALING CONSECUTIVE SQUARES (page 61)

Eleven consecutive squares form a spiral without
enclosing a hole, but adding the 12th square creates
a hole.

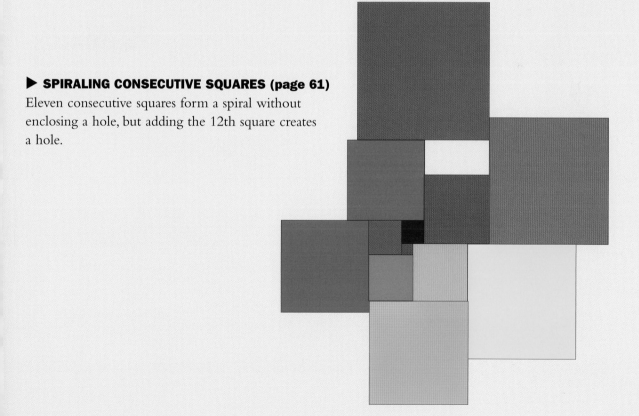

▼ CONSECUTIVE SQUARES TILING THE PLANE
(page 62)

One possible arrangement is shown.

▶ DODECAGON FROM
QUADRILATERALS
(page 63)

It should be noted that by adding 12 more pieces the dodecagon can be enlarged into a bigger dodecagon, and the pieces can tessellate the plane indefinitely.

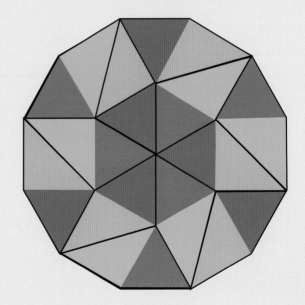

▼ **SMALLEST PERFECT RECTANGLE 1 (page 68)**

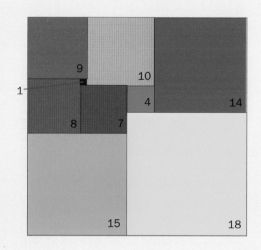

▼ **SMALLEST PERFECT RECTANGLE 2 (page 70)**

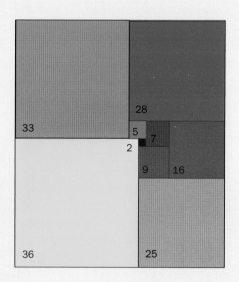

▼ **IMPERFECT SQUARE SPLIT (page 72)**

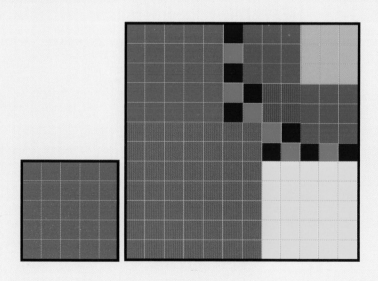

▼ INCOMPARABLE RECTANGLES (page 73)

The proportions of the smallest incomparably packed rectangle are 22 by 13 units.

The total area of the seven incomparable rectangles is 286 square units. Since one of the sides of the rectangle must be at least 18 units, and the sides must be integral, two possible proportions offer themselves:

26 by 11 units and 22 by 13 units.

The solution to our problem is the second, which has a smaller perimeter.

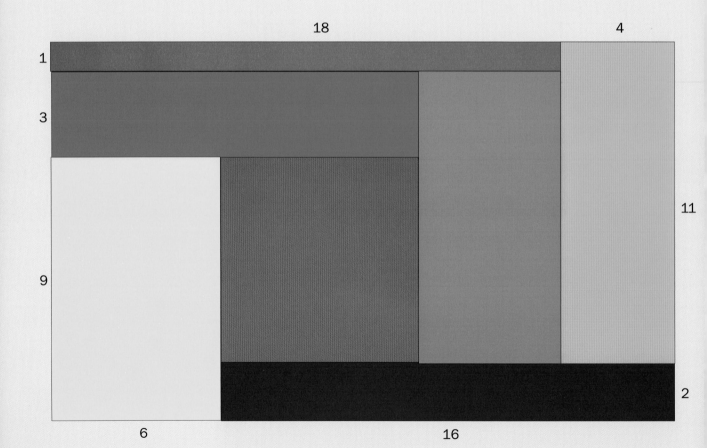

▼ **MORE IMPERFECT SQUARES (page 74)**

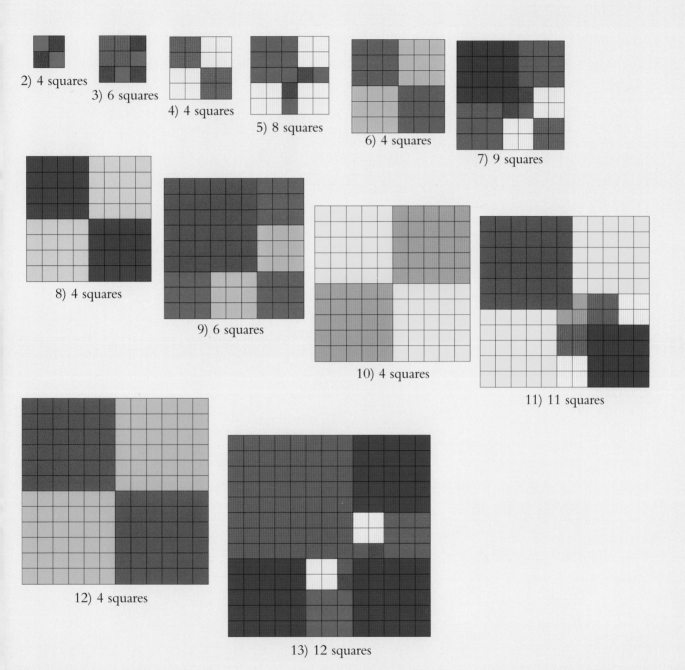

2) 4 squares

3) 6 squares

4) 4 squares

5) 8 squares

6) 4 squares

7) 9 squares

8) 4 squares

9) 6 squares

10) 4 squares

11) 11 squares

12) 4 squares

13) 12 squares

▼ **CUTTING CHOCOLATE (page 76)**

Six cuts as shown.

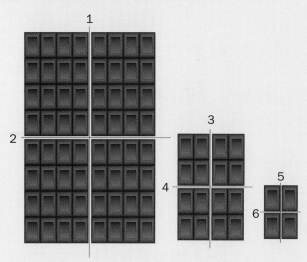

▼ **DODECAGON ZIGZAG (page 77)**

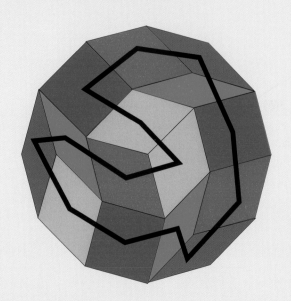

▼ **PACKING RECTANGLES (page 78)**

The 11 rectangles have the same total area as a 21-by-21 square. Will such a square be sufficient to contain the 11 rectangles?

My best efforts resulted in placing all but rectangle 6 (the 5-by-6 rectangle).

The 21-by-21 square cannot be fully covered by the 11 rectangles.

The smallest square in which all 11 rectangles will fit is a 22-by-22 square.

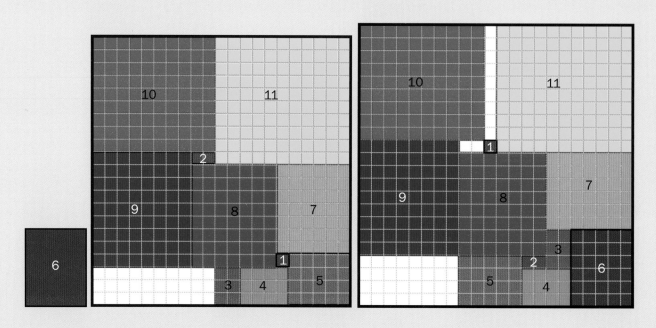

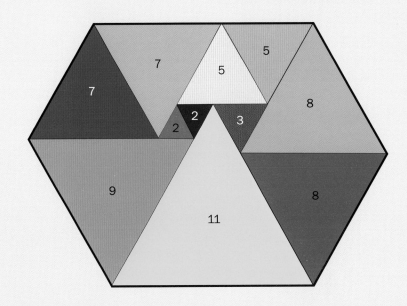

► **IMPERFECT HEXAGON (page 79)**

The smallest number of equilateral triangles into which the hexagon can be divided is 11 as shown.

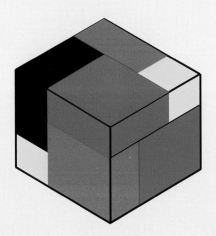

3-by-3 cube

◄ **THREE-BY-THREE CUBE PACKING (page 80)**

The usual intuitive way packing puzzles are attacked is to try to place the big pieces first, which is not always the correct strategy.

The secret of this puzzle is that the three small cubes have to be placed on one of the diagonals of the cube as shown. The bigger blocks can then be easily placed.

▼ **BOOKSHELF (page 81)**

1236 + 873 + 706 + 257 + 82 = 3154 add up exactly to the desired length.

While it is easy to add up five numbers to get 3154, it is not so easy to find those five numbers as a subset of a set of eight numbers.

Such a problem is a good example of how certain operations are very easy to carry out in one direction, but quite hard in reverse. This idea is used extensively in a new branch of cryptography called public-key cryptography.

▼ ROPE ACTS (page 82)

▶ **TRIANGULAR GARDEN (page 83)**

20 yards

▶ **STACKING WEIGHTS (page 84)**

▶ **GAIN AND LOSS (page 88)**

There is no magic involved. The pieces only seem to fit perfectly on the 63 and 65 unit grids. Small gaps between the pieces or slight overlaps account for the differences in area.

▼ **SPARE THE RECTANGLE (page 89)**

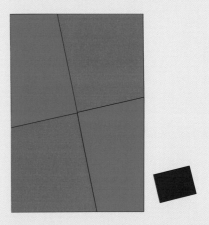

► CURRY'S PARADOX
(page 90)

Paul Curry, an amateur magician
in New York, created this
geometrical paradox in 1953.

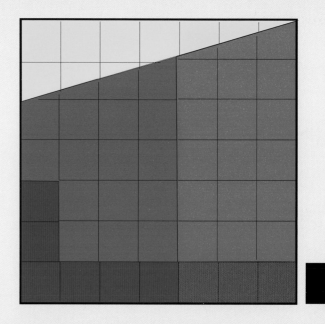

▼ CURRY'S TRIANGLE PARADOX (page 91)

▼ THE DISSAPPEARING SQUARE (pages 92 and 93)

The two squares seem to be identical, but as we have
learned, there are no miracles in geometry. The areas
of the two squares can't be equal. One of the squares
is certainly smaller, just not by much. It is of course
smaller by exactly as much as the area of the small
"superfluous" square which, as the result of the
ingenious transformation, is redistributed as a square
ring of negligible thickness around the border of the
puzzle. No wonder the smaller size of the big square
is not so obvious!

Puzzle 1   Puzzle 2

▼ TRIANGLE PARADOXES (page 94)

Real area: 69.5
Apparent area: 72

Real area: 70.5
Apparent area: 72

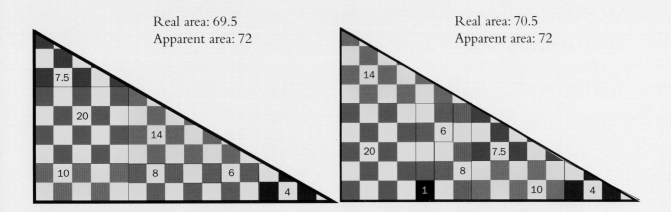

Real area: 71.5
Apparent area: 72

Real area: 72.5
Apparent area: 72

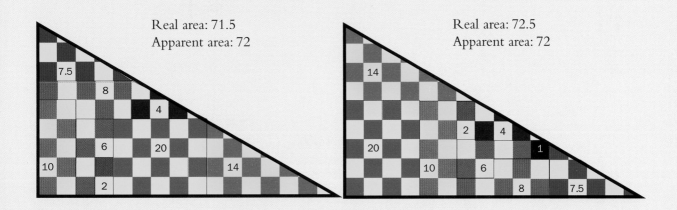

Real area: 73.5
Apparent area: 72

Real area: 74.5
Apparent area: 72

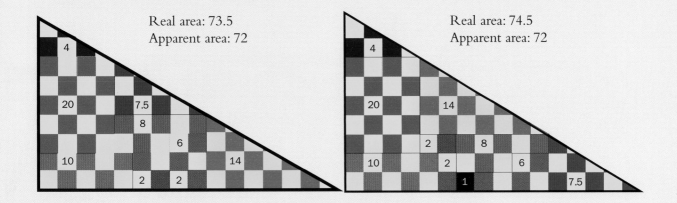

▼ CONSECUTIVE UNIQUE NUMBERS (page 96)

Puzzle 1 There are 90 2-digit numbers, as shown below:

Among them 8 numbers have consecutive digits, so the answer is 82 2-digit numbers.

10	11	12	13	14	15	16	17	18	19
20	21	22	23	24	25	26	27	28	29
30	31	32	33	34	35	36	37	38	39
40	41	42	43	44	45	46	47	48	49
50	51	52	53	54	55	56	57	58	59
60	61	62	63	64	65	66	67	68	69
70	71	72	73	74	75	76	77	78	79
80	81	82	83	84	85	86	87	88	89
90	91	92	93	94	95	96	97	98	99

Puzzle 2 There are 9 numbers in which the 2 digits are identical, so the answer is 81 2-digit numbers.

Puzzle 3 Maybe you are able to make the lengthy calculations in less than a minute. But it is enough to calculate the outcome once for any four-digit number, as you can see at right. You can do the same thing with numbers of up to 10 digits. The differences thus found are called unique numbers.

345	543 − 345 =	198
456	654 − 456 =	198
567	765 − 567 =	198
678	876 − 678 =	198
789	987 − 789 =	198
1234	4321 − 1234 =	3087
2345	5432 − 2345 =	3087
3456	6543 − 3456 =	3087
4567	7654 − 4567 =	3087
5678	8765 − 5678 =	3087
6789	9876 − 6789 =	3087

▶ HALF PACK (page 97)

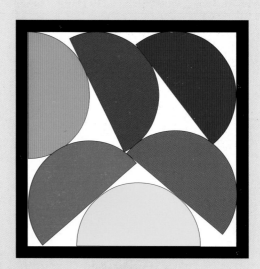